NO OTHER GODS

NO
OTHER
GODS

▼

THE POLITICS OF THE
TEN COMMANDMENTS

▲

ANA LEVY-LYONS

**CENTER
STREET**

New York Nashville

Center Street
Hachette Book Group
1290 Avenue of the Americas, New York, NY 10104
centerstreet.com
twitter.com/centerstreet

First Edition: March 2018

Center Street is a division of Hachette Book Group, Inc. The Center Street
name and logo are trademarks of Hachette Book Group, Inc.

The publisher is not responsible for websites (or their content)
that are not owned by the publisher.

The Hachette Speakers Bureau provides a wide range of authors for
speaking events. To find out more, go to www.hachettespeakersbureau.com
or call (866) 376-6591.

Translations from biblical Hebrew are by Ana Levy-Lyons.

Scripture quotations marked NSRV are from the New Revised Standard
Version Bible, copyright © 1989 the Division of Christian Education of the
National Council of the Churches of Christ in the United States of America.
Used by permission. All rights reserved.

Library of Congress Cataloging-in-Publication Data has been applied for.

ISBNs: 978-1-4789-7721-6 (hardcover), 978-1-4789-7720-9 (ebook)

Printed in the United States of America

LSC-C

10 9 8 7 6 5 4 3 2 1

To Jeff, my *beshert*

Contents

NO OTHER GODS

▼

The Ten Commandments Are Practices of Liberation

▲

A high school teacher of mine used to entertain his class by rattling off lists of oxymorons: pretty ugly, jumbo shrimp, constant variable. Sometimes he would take the opportunity to editorialize a little: military intelligence, airplane food, *liberal religion*. Everybody would smirk and the class would go on. The joke relied on the notion that liberal religion couldn't exist because liberals are not religious and religious people are definitely not liberal. As if everyone knows there's an inverse correlation between religiosity and liberalism: the more liberal you are, the less religious . . . to the vanishing point.

As with most jokes and stereotypes, there's some truth to it. If you look at any of the traditional markers of religiosity, religious liberals *are* less religious than the conservative or orthodox. Liberal Jews tend to not keep kosher; liberal Muslims tend to not pray five times a day; liberal Christians have been known to have premarital sex. As religions have liberalized and modernized, communal religious practices have fallen away. Religious fervor has cooled. The logic of this may seem obvious, but there is no necessary correlation between the substance of a person's theology and the amplitude of her religiosity. We have erroneously forged this correlation.

I thought of this a number of years ago when I was asked to lead an exercise with a group of religious liberals. I had asked them to imagine a community, based on their faith tradition, that was tight-knit, "really religious," and "really observant." I asked them to envision what foods members of this hypothetical community would eat, what they would wear, how they would raise their children, and how they would spend their time and money. What practices would be required? What would be prohibited?

Category by category, the response was the same: nothing would be required, nothing prohibited. I challenged them on this point: No foods would be prohibited? Not even foods grown by migrant farm workers for slave wages? Not even foods made through extreme cruelty to animals? Not even foods whose manufacturing pollutes rivers or accelerates climate change? Nothing prohibited? The response they consistently gave was that while people in this community would be inclined to, for example, avoid such foods, there would be no community-wide laws governing their practices. People would opt to do the right thing presumably because they would be good people who always try to do the right thing within reason.

Whether or not good people left to our own devices generally do the right thing is debatable. The world is awash with good people. Religious traditions have developed detailed ethical laws and elaborate technologies for remembering those laws precisely because, even for good people, doing the right thing consistently is hard. We need support and structure and a community around us to give us even a fighting chance. And sometimes doing the right thing "within reason" is not enough; sometimes doing the right thing means going beyond what feels comfortable or reasonable. Doing the right thing may mean acting in counterpoint to what the wider culture deems normal or acceptable. But clearly, to many religious liberals, what we ultimately do with our freedom of choice is of less concern than *that* we have this freedom. Yes, we value community and social justice and caring for the earth, but freedom is a higher value still.

Our Freedom Fetish

Our love of freedom has become a fetish. The honoring of individual freedom over communal flourishing is a ubiquitous and powerful norm in the United States among both progressives and conservatives, although in different ways. The trend in our culture has been inexorably toward a world of individuals, each doing his own thing. We elevate the self to an almost godlike status. This renders religion, in which the self is sublimated in the service of something larger, unpalatable at best.

One in five of us leave our birth religion, having found it soul-crushingly oppressive, mind-numbingly boring, or both. Increasingly we think of ourselves as "spiritual but not religious." We no longer rely on religious tradition for answers to life's big questions. We no longer feel that we need the Ten Commandments—or any commandments—in order to live an ethical life. We don't like being boxed in, we don't like being labeled, and we definitely do not like being "commanded."

But our triumphant world of freedom is failing us. It has not given us the personal fulfillment we seek. We have found ourselves adrift without a clear sense of purpose. Individualism has left us lonely. We spend longer and longer hours—cumulatively, even years—passively gazing at screens. Depression and anxiety are reaching epidemic proportions. "Deaths of despair"—deaths by suicide, opioids, and alcohol—are on the rise. When confronted with loss and suffering, we reach for rituals that once held meaning, only to find them empty, strange, and incongruous with our lives. We resort to "retail therapy." We have done ourselves a disservice by choosing freedom *from* religion and going no further in our seeking. We've refused the cumulative spiritual wisdom of the millennia. We've drifted into the moral and spiritual shallows. When anything goes, it's hard to actually go deep.

Our lack of spiritual grounding has not only impoverished us individually; it has global consequences. Environmental devastation, economic injustice, and the pervasive violence of our society are made possible by our mass acquiescence to the systems that propel them. Through countless tiny, daily, socially sanctioned acts, we reflexively create and re-create those systems. When we are spiritually vulnerable, we can't help but participate in them. We can't even imagine living differently. When we are isolated, communities are fragmented, and we have no shared sense of religious purpose; we lose the will to resist the wrongs we see around us. We feel powerless to do anything about them. We become anesthetized to the suffering in our world and we lack any outside vantage point from which to envision a better one. So we worship "other gods"—wealth, power, the approval of others, and the eternal spectacle served up on our screens—and these other gods gain unbridled power. This is the political moment in which we find ourselves today.

The greatest irony is that the postreligious world has not granted us its promised freedom. While it seems like we can now do "whatever we want," what we want is often invisibly shaped by powers beyond our awareness. There is always *something* that guides our aspirations— something for which we are willing to sacrifice. If we do not decide what that "something" is, it will be decided for us by the indifferent forces of the commercial marketplace. An observation on this point often attributed to Ralph Waldo Emerson reads,

> Truly, the gods we worship write their names on our faces. A person will worship something— have no doubt about that. We may think our tribute is paid in secret in the dark recesses of our hearts—but it will out. That which dominates our imaginations and our thoughts will determine our lives, and character. Therefore, it behooves us to be careful what we worship, for what we are worshipping, we are becoming.

We may feel today that we've outgrown the need for the religious strictures of the past. But those very strictures might well have been devised for exactly such a moment as this. Now may be when we need them most. *Especially* today, we need shared commitments to hold ourselves accountable to history, to the future, to one another, and to something larger than all of us.

We need faith in our collective power to transform the world toward justice—a power authorized and fueled by the ground of being itself. Choose-your-own-adventure spirituality is inadequate to the challenges we face. We need religious practices like the Ten Commandments that are rooted in a deep and multilayered tradition, that are spiritually rich, and that are intentionally insulated from modern culture.

Okay, Okay, but Why All the Rules?

Many of us concede that we need to do something to cool the feverish pace of our high-tech lives. We want a greater sense of community and connection. We know that we should try to carve out more "me" time or more time with our families. And perhaps we should give more to charity or do more to work for justice and healing in our world. But we are understandably skeptical about rules. Getting mired in arcane religious protocols seems counterproductive. Since we already reject some of the laws of religious traditions, why should we submit to any religious laws at all? If we should be free to marry someone of our same gender or to have sex before marriage, surely we should be free to do more seemingly trivial things like run an errand on a Sunday or eat a cheeseburger.

When talking about Sabbath rules, for example, here is what some of my congregants tell me:

> "I do a Sabbath a little bit at a time—an hour here, an hour there. But I don't want anyone to tell me when to do it."

> "I take time off when I can, but sometimes it's just not feasible."

> "I prefer to just try to keep a Sabbath vibe—feeling connected with my higher power—all the time, not just once a week."

These are all ways of claiming that we are in control of our lives, our time, our choices. We are like the alcoholic who says, "I can stop anytime." But for most of us it's not that easy. The chronic anxiety with which so many of us live our lives today belies that claim. Our national epidemics of obesity and anorexia, drug addiction, and stress-related disorders in children and adults belie that claim. And our global runaway train of environmental destruction belies that claim. We are not in control.

We underestimate the tremendous, invisible power of our culture—the addictive pull of producing and consuming and the massive pressure to conform to social norms. We underestimate the capacity of the media (social and broadcast) to induce self-loathing—the feeling that we are never good enough. The seemingly perfect, glowing, beautiful families on Facebook and the ingenious ads for the latest shampoo or smartphone steadily feed our insecurities. And when we contemplate a full, committed religious practice, we quail at the social costs we would pay. For many of us, the whispered voices of fear are loud in our ears warning of our world spinning out of control, the threat of inadequacy and failures.

The cycle of producing and consuming is literally addictive and can often be pleasurable, yet it doesn't begin to exhaust the spectacular range of human experience and depth of meaning available to us. When we revolve forever in its orbit, we'll never know what we're missing. And we'll never know for sure whether we can, in fact, "stop anytime" until we try. If we're serious about reaching escape velocity, we need to bring some serious counterforce. The Ten Commandments can serve as that counterforce.

Just as secular culture offers freedom from religion's laws, religious law offers freedom from secular culture's laws. The question is not, *Should we be bound by law or should we be free?* The question is, *In which law are we most unduly or unhappily bound? And in which freedom are we most truly free?*

Wrestling with Old-Time Religion

Not everyone, of course, has embraced modernity's freedom from religion with enthusiasm. Some, like Lynn Westmoreland, a Republican congressman from Georgia, want to turn back the clock and promote commandments, a clear list of right and wrong, a set moral code. A number of years ago, Westmoreland agreed to go on *The Colbert Report* to be interviewed. He had been actively working to get the Ten Commandments installed in all courthouses in the United States. In the course of the interview, he explained, "The Ten Commandments is not a bad thing for people to understand and to respect. Where better place could you have something like that than in a judicial building?"

Colbert, in his inimitable way, replied, "That's an excellent question. Can you think of any better building to put the Ten Commandments in than in a public building?"

Westmoreland said, "No."

Then Colbert asked, "What are the Ten Commandments?"

Westmoreland looked like he had been hit by a two-by-four. "What are all of 'em? You want me to name 'em all?"

He couldn't do it. For Westmoreland, the Ten

Commandments collectively have cultural meaning that far outweighs their content. The Ten Commandments in public buildings would legitimate the values of his culture, which are not identical to the values of the Ten Commandments. If the content were what mattered, he would know what the content was.

The Ten Commandments are used and abused in many ways for many different agendas. Like the Bible itself, they are a Rorschach test at this point, often revealing more about their viewer than about their own content. Conservative Christians like Westmoreland use them as a banner of so-called "traditionalism." Orthodox Jews extrapolate their meaning through long chains of legalistic reasoning, such that there is now a cottage industry of devices that allow a person to, for example, use a food processor on a Saturday by flipping a switch that *breaks* an electronic circuit, thus avoiding "lighting a fire," and thereby keeping the letter of the Sabbath commandment.

The spiritual-but-not-religious, on the other hand, make wry jokes and demote the Ten Commandments to the "ten suggestions." Atheists like Sam Harris relegate them, and religion generally, to the "cesspool of mythology." For many of us modern people in affluent nations, the commandments are a symbol of oppression, misogyny, and tribalism. They smell musty and old, cranky and inflexible. They've become linked with dogmatic, chauvinistic zeal. "You shall not kill" is used in antiabortion rhetoric. "You shall not commit adultery" is used in anti-gay rhetoric. This is a chilling association to those who have been hurt by conservative legislation or even personal attacks from the religious far right. Some of the commandments make sense to us; some seem arbitrary. At best, they seem to be self-evident ethical guidelines that require no religious imprimatur. But we reject their authority and religious authority generally.

In our cultural imagination, there seem to be only two options for relating to religious traditions like the Ten Commandments: either embrace them as they are understood by social conservatives like Lynn Westmoreland or write them off as irredeemable and abandon them. Rabbi Eliezer Diamond, a professor at the Jewish Theological Seminary in New York City, offers a beautiful third alternative. He acknowledges the oppressive religious structures against which progressives have justifiably rebelled. Then he urges us not to abandon sacred texts because of how past generations have interpreted them. Rather, we should explore deeper to find the kernel of revelation buried within them.

The following passage suggests how feminists could interact with blatantly misogynist scriptural texts. The same principle could apply for anyone tempted to write off the Bible or religion entirely.

> The...wholesale rejection of the corpus of biblical and rabbinic writings as irredeemably misogynous is an oversimplification that cuts women off from the trans-generational conversation that has been created and sustained for thousands of years. I would argue that...[the study of the Torah should] include a version of the *mitzvah of pidyon shvuyim*, the traditional name for the commandment to redeem those held in captivity against their will. Indeed, by redeeming those passages and teachings of the Torah that are held captive by narrowness of vision, and by understanding that narrowness to be a function of the time and place in which they were formulated... we can breathe new life into texts that may seem dead to us.

In other words, Diamond teaches that the beautiful, truly inspired spiritual wisdom contained in the Bible is being "held captive" by the constraints of the time and place of its authors. It's buried. It's our job to excavate it, to set it free and give it new life for our day. It contains profound teachings for us. We are called to add our voices to that transgenerational conversation. Rather than cede the sole right of interpretation to the authorities of the past, we are empowered, by virtue of our spiritual inheritance as human beings, to contribute our own insights and vision, to separate out what is truly inspired from what is just a product of a particular historical moment. Rather than reject these ancient traditions sight unseen, we are invited to reclaim them.

And we should be very careful when consigning anything to the trash bin of history because we too are held captive by the constraints of *our* time and place. We know more than the ancients in some ways but we must remain open to the possibility that they may know more than we in others.

What Don't We Eat?

Everyone is struggling to find meaning in our secular age. Many of us who have rejected traditional religion are spiritually hungry nonetheless. A congregant of mine told me a story of her son, adopted from Ethiopia, who was trying to understand his new family's religion. He had come to her and said, "My friend Ahmed at school is Muslim and his family doesn't drink alcohol; Hannah is Jewish and her family doesn't eat pork; what don't *we* eat?" The mother wanted to be able to give him an answer, but she couldn't. I remembered again that group of religious liberals who insisted that there be nothing that they, for religious reasons, don't eat.

But many of us want meaningful answers to questions like this boy's—meaningful practices to help us live in light of our values. We crave a spiritual grounding for our political commitments and a way to connect our day-to-day lives to something larger than ourselves. We yearn for connection to a sense of history and a thread of continuity with tradition—to integrate the present and the past in a way that feels meaningful.

Religion has served as a bulwark of meaning in American society since Europeans began landing on these shores in the sixteenth century, and for native peoples since long before that. It has provided an overarching context whereby our actions in this life translate to the realm of ideals and spirit. Rituals of marriage and coming of age engender real, felt transformations. Acts of religious virtue—compassionate care, charity, and defending an ideal of the good—allow us to participate in divine work. Religion has been the primary social structure for the vast majority of Americans and it has grounded our communities for centuries. It has given us a holistic understanding of our shared human experience.

This stabilizing role of religion is well-known and

has furnished religion with its reputation (leveraged by my high school teacher in his oxymoron joke) as a conservative force in society. But religion has also historically been a disruptive, countercultural force. In our day, it is this more radical edge of religion—proactive and passionate—that we need. At its best, religion provides an "outside" to the socially constructed world. Through religion, we can discover another place to be—a vantage point of imagination from which to see reality, critique society, and change what some believe can't be changed. Along with visionary clergy throughout history, we can read the Hebrew Bible as a politically radical manifesto, teaching the sharing of wealth, stewardship of the earth, and freedom from materialism. Through embracing its disciplines of spiritually engaged collective practice, we can gain moral authority in the public sphere. And we can all be called to a life of meaning.

The Ten Commandments are a resource for resistance. They are a politically and spiritually brazen prescription—one which, if actually followed, would turn our world upside down. Far from being merely a vestigial remnant of an oppressive era (though they are that) and far from being a simple rehearsal of ethical norms on which we already agree (though they are, on one level, that too), the Commandments are countercultural practices. They offer a bold spiritual consciousness in which we commit ourselves unconditionally to the force in the universe that makes transformation and love possible. We don't have to invent a bunch of new practices for a meaningful way to live out our spirituality and politics. There is a perfectly good set of ten of them, all ready to go, with as much progressive firepower as any of us can handle, that has existed for some three thousand years.

Practices of Liberation

This book is a work of midrash—a Jewish interpretive tradition that seeks to distill spiritual meaning from a Torah text. (The Torah is the central text of the Hebrew scriptures, called the "Old Testament" by Christians. I also use the word "midrash" throughout the book to refer to stories and interpretations drawn from the body of rabbinic writings about the commandments.) In keeping with postmodern etiquette, I do not claim that my interpretation of the Ten Commandments text is what it "actually" means or what its author meant. No one can know for sure the intention of people writing millennia ago. But I do claim a faith that in and among the parts of the Torah that are merely reflections of an ancient place and time, there is a through line of profound spiritual and political insight. The commandments are a channel for revelation. Each generation can set the text against the backdrop of its experience and find meaning.

The Ten Commandments were first written in ancient Hebrew on parchment or papyrus scrolls somewhere between 1400 and 586 BCE. They were undoubtedly circulating as part of the oral tradition of the Hebrew people long before they were written down, parts of them also having been borrowed from other peoples in the ancient Near East. They appear in slightly different versions in Exodus and Deuteronomy. While they are not the only commandments in the Torah—rabbis have identified a total of 613 commandments—they occupy a special place in the canon for Jews and Christians. The Hebrew word used to describe them—*devarim*—is notably not "commandments." More literal translations are "things" or "words" or "utterances." I gloss them as "concepts" or even "blessings."

Even more important for our purposes than the historical context of the Ten Commandments is their context within the sacred mythology of the Torah itself. The revelation of the Ten Commandments comes at a critical moment in the Exodus story. The Israelites had been liberated from slavery in Egypt just three months earlier, escaping through the parted waters of the Sea of Reeds (Red Sea) with Moses leading them. When they emerge in freedom on the other side, they don't know what to do with their freedom. They wander around the desert, sniping at each other and disobeying God multiple times. Finally ready to receive this public revelation, they assemble at the foot of Mount Sinai and Moses tells them to prepare themselves spiritually for three days. They are to wash themselves and their clothes and refrain from sex. If they so much as touch the base of the mountain, the electric charge will be too strong and they will die.

Before this moment, Moses had always been their prophetic messenger, relaying God's messages. This time is different. The whole mountain goes up in smoke, flames, and thunder and God speaks the commandments out loud directly to the people. For the first time, they receive a definition of God and a systematic description of their relationship with God. The sensory and spiritual overload is described as terrifying and overwhelming (as one midrash tells it, when the Israelites heard that "awful" voice, they "flew back in their horror twelve miles"). When God finishes speaking, the people beg Moses to not make them hear directly from God ever again. They say, "Don't let God speak with us or we will die!" Moses agrees to resume his place as the intermediary and goes up the mountain, "drawing near into the thick darkness where God was." God engraves the Ten Commandments with God's own finger on two stone tablets.

That the context of the Ten Commandments is so foreign to many of us today is part of what makes them a potent resource. They were written in a very different time in a language that is strange and terse and rich in symbolism and mythic archetypes. They exist outside of our social context (even as they were conceived within a social context of their own). Our hyperconnected world under global capitalism is different from that of nomadic desert economies millennia ago. Life and people are different. Unlike the Hebrew people, who were essentially tribal, we know very few of the people whom we affect. The keeping and breaking of commandments for us takes different forms and has further-reaching impacts. Today we can kill and steal indirectly as well as directly. Today we can make and worship idols collectively without even knowing it. Today we can lie and that lie can change reality.

And yet the human predilections and struggles that the commandments engage are recognizable and resonant to us today. Today's world is as mythically epic, in its own way, as that of the Exodus. The ultrawealthy are giants more powerful than the ancient Pharaoh of Egypt. Corporate powers play the role of gods who can determine the fate of millions and alter the forces of nature no less dramatically than the ten plagues in Egypt or the parting of the Sea of Reeds. Our time has its own great narratives of oppression and liberation. The Ten Commandments give us an outside vantage point from which to truly see them. When read in this way, the social and political critiques embedded in the text practically jump off the page. And the constraints and disciplines that they require of us become revealed for what they really are: practices of liberation.

YHVH

▼

The First Commandment

You Shall Have No Other Gods besides Me

▲

Dethrone the Modern Deities of Political, Social, and Corporate Power

I am YHVH, your God, who brought you out from the land of Egypt, from a house of slaves. You shall have no other gods besides me.

It's almost as if the movie came first. The setting could not be more cinematic: a desert mountain shrouded in smoke, a booming voice traveling down to the people below amid lightning, thunder, and quaking earth. The voice begins by introducing itself out loud to the trembling crowd with a startling revelation: "I am YHVH, your God."

Some commentators say that the story could have stopped right there—roll the credits—that every commandment and all subsequent spiritual wisdom tumbles directly and inevitably out of this one truth.

YHVH—that which identifies itself as "your God" in this biblical text—is the Roman alphabet rendering of the Hebrew verb "to be." In other words, Being itself is addressing us, humanity, as "your God." It's not a big man in the sky or a big woman or a big anything. It is not any one particular force of nature, like the sun or the rain, as were some of the gods in the ancient Near East. The word YHVH is temporally, spatially, and grammatically nonspecific—it could be translated as "is" or "will be" or "am becoming" or "have become" or "has been" or "could be" or any other form that expresses the state of *being*. This is a God without boundaries. It is the bare face of reality itself.

The letters are written without any vowels so we have no hint as to how to pronounce it—and in Jewish tradition its pronunciation is not meant to be even attempted. Even the consonants *y*, *h*, and *v* are open sounds, associated with air and breath, not definition or finality. YHVH is considered the most sacred name of God—unpronounceable because it stands for something unfathomable.

YHVH is all that is known and unknown. It is past, present, future, and beyond time. It is infinite space, matter, and nothingness. It is all the natural systems of the earth, laws of physics, and biological processes. It is all the people we love. We can only imagine in that breathtaking moment how the name YHVH, spoken in first person, might have sounded. Perhaps it was like wind; perhaps it was like a sine wave or an ocean wave or a vibration or a heartbeat.

And perhaps none of this ever happened. Perhaps all of this dramatic description of a revelation of Being itself, spoken from a seething mountaintop, is a mytho-poetic way of transposing the experience of enlightenment. From this perspective, where God is not "a being" but "being itself," the first commandment has an Eastern spiritual flavor. A Buddhist teacher might rephrase it: We shall have no "gods," meaning deities with a white picket fence perimeter that are really just projections of our own minds anyway. Instead we shall practice seeing things as they are and embracing what is. We sit and we breathe (*y-h-v-h*) and our breath connects us with reality on the rawest, most primal level. With this interpretation, anytime we think we've found a way to define God or understand reality intellectually, we are wrong; hence Zen master Linji's famous koan, "If you meet the Buddha in the road, kill him." The truth is too big to be contained in any human concept.

And in a direct echo of the first commandment and the prohibition against pronouncing the name of YHVH, the Tao Te Ching opens with the sentence, "The Tao that can be named is not the eternal Tao." Anything small enough to be named, anything limited in any way, shall not be a god for you. Keep your eye on the ball, the real thing—the *only* real thing: reality.

The God of Liberation

If this were the exhaustive meaning of the first commandment, it would be a wise spiritual teaching, but it would be apolitical and amoral. The concept of YHVH would be empty of any qualities or characteristics. YHVH would have no stake in human events because it would equally saturate all dimensions of any given situation. It would be pure consciousness, sitting cross-legged, watching in equanimity as worlds rise and fall and then get thrown into the cosmic blender and rise again. Life and death would be equivalent from its perspective. Justice and injustice would have no meaning. The practice of seeing YHVH/reality would be purely the practice of seeing what *is*, without judgment.

But in the Torah, the concept of YHVH is far from empty. YHVH is introduced at the start of the Ten Commandments as a very particular dimension of reality, with a very particular role in human history: "I am YHVH, your God, *who brought you out from the land of Egypt, from a house of slaves.*" It's a stunning description. YHVH could have been described in so many ways... as the God who made the world or the God who judges human beings or the God who makes the sun rise or the earth spin. But no. YHVH is identified as the starring actor in the struggle for freedom from slavery. The one thing we are to know about this God—the one defining characteristic—is that this is the God of liberation, the *power* of liberation itself, that which brings us from injustice to justice.

YHVH is not just existence as a static fact, but existence as something in particular: the power of life expanding and making it possible for us all to expand from our places of constriction. YHVH is not impartial or disinterested. In the Exodus story invoked here, YHVH acted on behalf of an oppressed people against a militarized, imperial, unjust power. They were a people who had committed acts of resistance and civil disobedience to try to right the wrongs they had encountered. (When the Pharaoh ordered the midwives to kill all male Israelite babies as soon as they were born, the midwives didn't do it. When Moses saw an Egyptian beating an Israelite slave, Moses killed the Egyptian.) God acted on behalf of a people who were a minority in their land, a people who were enslaved and abused, a people who were powerless. This story of resistance, struggle, and liberation is the central story in the Torah and the heart of the Ten Commandments. This God of liberation is our God.

The Chaise Lounge of Social Norms

None of this is new theological territory. Liberation theology in Latin America, black theology and womanist theology in the United States, Dalit theology of the "untouchables" in India, Palestinian liberation theology, as well as contemporary Jewish theologies and others around the world draw from the Exodus story as well as the Hebrew prophets, the Jesus story, and other biblical traditions. They find in the texts a God with a special concern for the poor and the oppressed. They draw strength from stories of a God so powerful and so passionately committed to the marginalized, that it overturns the laws of nature on their behalf time and again. God grants small rebel forces victory over great armies, parts the sea, and even raises the persecuted prophet from the dead. The powerless prevail over the powerful. Most Jewish and Christian holidays exist to celebrate these victories (netted out as, "They tried to kill us. We survived. Let's eat").

And yet, despite all the lucid and inspired teachings about the God of liberation, the religious right casts God as the white patriarch and the enforcer of human hierarchies. They paint a God that would more likely have been the mascot of Pharaoh's army than the liberator of slaves. They ignore the political radicalism of the biblical stories and insist that we will have to wait for the afterlife to see justice. Some Christians argue that religion is a private, internal, spiritual matter—a personal relationship with Jesus Christ (disregarding Jesus' own public, prophetic ministry). Some Jewish orthodoxies maintain that following the letter of the law is the essence of the religious life—arcane rules about how an animal's blood is handled, for example, have more bearing on kashrut (dietary law) than the conditions under which that animal lived or the impact of its life on the earth that God created. Such blinkered theology allows the religious right to maintain a cozy alliance with the political right and with the economic status quo. Religion reclines comfortably in the chaise lounge of social norms.

The first commandment calls us into a more oppositional relationship with cultural conventions and political powers. And it spans the public and private realms. In order to "keep" this commandment, we first need to know YHVH, know "other gods," and be able to tell the difference.

We then need to place YHVH—the power of liberation—at the center of our lives and demote all "other gods" to nongod status, where they belong.

This is a tall order in our culture, where secular norms dictate how we should prioritize our time and our money, where billions are spent marketing other gods to us in the form of brands, and where military and corporate powers are so genuinely massive as to feel godlike.

To resist all of this requires a full body, full soul, unmediated engagement with our world—one in which the spiritual and the political are truly one and the same. The wording of the commandment, which is usually translated into English as "you shall have no other gods," is more directly translated as "there shall *be* for you no other gods." In other words, other things shall not even begin to exist as gods in our lives. We won't worship them, we won't look to them for salvation, we won't depend on them to fill the aching loneliness in our hearts, we won't work for them, we won't serve them, we won't give up our power to them.

One *Mitzrayim*, One Struggle, One Liberation

According to the Jewish mystical text called the Zohar, the Hebrew word for Egypt, Mitzrayim, also means a narrow place, a place of constriction, boundaries, or limits. The name of Pharaoh, then, the great villain of the Exodus story who is called Melech Mitzrayim, can be translated as "King of Constriction." The whole story can be read on two levels: as a political exodus of a people from slavery and as an allegory of spiritual constriction and liberation—an internal enslavement by our internal oppressors with whom we suffer, struggle, and eventually prevail. We are born into a new life through the birth canal of the parted waters of the sea. So the God who brings us out from the land of Egypt is also the God who gives us the heart to battle our internal demons, the courage to do the things that terrify us, the power to overcome our addictions, and the strength to love better than we ourselves were loved.

The story of the Israelites enslaved in Egypt stands for every story of oppression around the world, and the story of their God-fueled liberation is every liberation. YHVH is with the Indian farmers impoverished by free trade with affluent nations; YHVH is with the alcoholic struggling for another day of sobriety; YHVH is with the indigenous Canadians whose islands are being destroyed by climate change; YHVH is with the young black man subjected to discrimination, police violence, and another year in prison. The God who brings us out from a house of slaves is the God who gives individuals the power to break free from their deepest and most private oppressions and gives communities the power to break free from the systemic oppressions of our day. It's one God operating on many registers. The first commandment teaches that we are to have no gods but that one.

It's not just that this commandment is both spiritual and political, or even that the spiritual and the political are intertwined. The genius of this commandment is that it reveals how the spiritual and the political are mutually generative. Every private and spiritual struggle exists in a political context. The homeless veteran suffering from PTSD can perhaps someday find a place to live, escape the nightmares, and get back on his feet, but the liberation is only complete when the social conditions that caused the collapse of his dreams have been overturned for everyone. Any attempt to keep this commandment teaches us that we will never be free spiritually until we are free politically and materially. And vice versa. It is all one *mitzrayim*, one struggle, and one liberation. And in that struggle, we have the greatest possible power at our disposal. The audacious premise of the Ten Commandments is that reality (YHVH) is not neutral: it bends toward the marginalized and the powerless. In the struggle for justice, life itself has a dog in the fight.

Other Gods

What "other gods" do we have today? Most of us could do a quick scan of our lives and admit that we have pretty much all of 'em. We have the obvious ones—the god of money, the god of power, the god of prestige and success, the god of pleasure. We have the less obvious ones—the god of culturally defined beauty, the god of what-other-people-think, the god of getting-to-choose, and the god of how-things-have-always-been. We may have the god of our children (the worship of which has been aptly termed "descendant worship"), our high school, our team, our country, or our race. The worship of such gods is ultimately self-aggrandizement—loyalty to a given group for no other reason than that one happens to be a member of it; it is ultimately the worship of the god of the self. And we have our very private, secret other gods—a parent's voice in our heads, a fear of failure, a fear of success, alcohol or other drugs, a drive toward self-destruction, or simply another person.

These other gods in our lives, usually several overlapping and vying for dominance, demand from us various forms of supplication. The god of the male gaze may demand that a woman pay a monthly tribute of physical pain and money as she gets her legs waxed and spend weeks of her life every year managing her hair and her nails, applying and removing makeup, choosing clothes that display "assets" and hide "flaws." The god of money may demand that a broker sell a mortgage to someone he knows won't be able to afford it and won't be able to refinance once the ARM kicks in and the interest rate doubles. The god of power may demand that a politician fight against a bill to keep coal ash (the by-product of burning coal) out of the drinking water supplies for poor communities. The god of "my country" may demand that we build walls and tear families apart to keep foreigners out.

Some of us might say that when we do things like indulge in beauty rituals, we aren't worshipping "other gods"; we are freely choosing how we want to live our lives. Or that when we sell subprime mortgages, we are simply being ambitious and doing our job and, anyway, no one's forcing anyone to buy. Maybe these things for which we are so lavishly rewarded by our society just happen to be our preferences. Maybe they are empowering expressions of our true selves. And of course this is hypothetically possible. Some of us could just happen to enjoy having a hairless bikini line and some of us could just happen to like selling mortgages even when they harm people, and our choices could have nothing to do with social expectations, the workings of power, the influence of media, the cultural constructions of gender, and all the immense pressures on us to do these very things. But that would be quite a coincidence.

Many other gods masquerade as priorities that we ourselves choose and, in fact, as elements that enrich our lives. Convenience, for example, is another other god widely worshipped in American culture. We will take plastic bags for our groceries, drive our SUV somewhere that a bus could take us, stick our kids in front of a violent TV show, and buy bottled water instead of bringing a bottle from home even when our values might dictate different choices for all of these. Where our lives might otherwise be rife with indignities we can't avoid and compromises we feel obliged to make, we feel eminently entitled to convenience.

Sports is another example. Professional athletes are openly worshipped in this society and sports fans rarely balk at their multi-million-dollar salaries or the oceanic resources used and waste generated in each game. The reverence for the game and its players trickles down to amateur and high school athletics as well, where winners are lauded as heroes and no amount of attention or support for their training is too much. Above all, *they* must never be inconvenienced. Professional athletics is a $60 billion–per-year industry while, according to UN estimates, it would take only half that much annually to eliminate world hunger. The other gods are woven deeply and often invisibly into our consciousness.

The Tyranny of "Balance"

The greatest and most powerful of other gods in American culture is that of business. The freedom of corporations to make money is held as a sacred imperative that supersedes all other values. It supersedes the right of workers to make a salary that can keep them out of poverty. It supersedes the right of consumers to know what they are buying and protect their health. By its essential nature it pillages the earth and exploits the animals on it, superseding the rights of entire species and ecosystems to exist.

"Balance" is the euphemism most commonly used to justify such exploitation of people and the earth: we must "balance" the interests of business with other interests. But what meaning can "balance" have when what is sitting on one side of the hanging scales is, for example, the likely annihilation of all ocean life through the seafood industry? Or the gruesome death of a commercial fishing worker with small children at home (fishing being the most dangerous occupation in the US)? What could possibly balance such losses? The most direct manifestation of YHVH is the natural world, including humans, that precipitated out from it. To subject the natural world and its creatures to the tyranny of "balance" with the interests of business is to baldly worship an other god to devastating effect.

Middle-class people in affluent nations tend to think that we at least have a choice in what other gods we worship and to what extent we worship them. We believe that we personally strike a reasonable "balance" in how we order our priorities and where we focus our attention. We might compare ourselves to people in developing nations or poor people in our own who are materially trapped and have no possibility of balance. Their other gods are real powers outside of themselves that they have no realistic option but to obey. An undocumented immigrant has no choice but to open the door when Immigration and Customs Enforcement (ICE) shows up with a judicial warrant. A destitute Brazilian farmer has no choice but to burn acres of the Amazon to make a living. Our other gods, by contrast, are just "in our heads." We don't actually have to do what they say.

Yet the vast majority of the time, we *do* do what they say. The lives of those of us with "choice" are completely out of actual balance. The so-called choices we have made, and continue to make, are driving our planet to the brink of its ability to support life as we know it. And while the average American SUV driver, business executive, or football fan certainly has far greater social and economic resources than the average undocumented immigrant or Brazilian farmer, it would be underestimating the power of other gods to say that their power exists only in our heads.

To defy the other gods is to incur very real costs. For a woman to go to the office with hairy legs or without makeup looks less professional. It can be career limiting. It can be relationship limiting. We shave and primp not so much for the sake of beauty, but for the sake of normalcy. For a man to give up a high-paying job or eschew sports or wear secondhand clothes to work or use awkward work-arounds to avoid plastic bags or bottles could mean losing the esteem of his peers. It could expose him to an unbearable level of vulnerability. It could mean losing his place in the world. For a female executive to accept lower profit margins for her division in the name of an ethical initiative could cost her the job—in a corporate world where professional women are still struggling to gain purchase. These are real costs. Such is the power of other gods.

Demoting Other Gods

For all these reasons, the work of disentangling YHVH— the life-sustaining and liberating forces within us— from other gods is an extraordinary challenge. It is the private and public work of a lifetime. Growing up in any given culture, we are constructed by the gods of that culture on a foundational level. Social confirmation of the power of those other gods confronts us everywhere we turn. And the towering figures and voices from our childhood traumas act as yet *other* other gods in our lives, for many of us until the day we die. The practice of keeping the first commandment, then, is first a practice of ongoing discernment—exploring our own motivations for the things we do, even the things, or *especially* the things, that seem most mundane. And it is the spiritual work of questioning the assumptions of the very political and social worlds in which we are most deeply immersed, as well as those of our families and our most intimate relationships. This is best done in the context of a community with a tradition of religious resistance.

In this daunting task, it's important to remember that the first commandment does not require us to give up the things that we currently care most about (once we have figured out what they are). It does not require us to give up trying to look attractive or making money or enjoying sports or great food. It requires us to not allow these things to *be gods* for us. It requires us to dethrone them in our lives.

The first commandment requires us to elevate YHVH. This means that when we're thinking about the quality and purpose of our lives over time, we think first and foremost of how we can be of service in the liberation of the oppressed and in protecting the natural abundance of YHVH on this earth. These are our first considerations when making long-term career choices and immediate consumer choices; our first considerations in how we speak to our peers, bosses, employees, families, children; how we treat animals and what we do for fun.

And while the point of this commandment is not deprivation—far from it!—to elevate YHVH and the process of liberation will necessarily entail significant "lifestyle" changes for most of us. This can be a difficult or even painful transition. The standard American diet, for example, directly conflicts with the protection of our ecosystems and the people who depend on them. But the food we eat is "normal," by definition; it's pleasurable; it connects us with family, friends, and the larger society; it's convenient; it's deeply ingrained and layered with meaning. And so even *talking* about changing what we eat can provoke a fight-or-flight response in some of us.

The same goes for questioning what kinds of entertainment we pay for, whom we aim to please through our work, and how much stuff we consider to be enough stuff to own. For some of us, depending on our social position, this process itself can be liberating. It can be the joyful work of discovering our true selves and finding our real God. For others, especially those of us who are more privileged or happily ensconced in society, it can be the practice of biting the hand that feeds us.

The Asymptotic Practice of Realignment

In geometry, an asymptote is a curved line approaching a straight line at just such an angle that the two lines get closer and closer but never actually touch...at least not in finite space. Keeping the first commandment is like this—a process of gradual realignment, curving closer and closer to YHVH but never, in our finite lives, touching. As we discover the activities of other gods in our lives like blurry images coming into focus, it is the practice of consciously making choices, bit by bit, each day, to loosen their grip and align our lives with life-sustaining liberation. And as we see the operations of other gods in our society more and more clearly, it is the political work of resisting those oppressive powers and working toward policies of liberation and compassion. We will never get all the way there in one lifetime. Perhaps if we did, that would be the experience of enlightenment—a complete oneness with Being itself. Perhaps that would be like the moment of hearing the name of YHVH directly, spoken in first person from the mountaintop.

But we can undertake a committed, if asymptotic, journey. And while we may have to give up a great deal on this journey, we may also find that there is a great deal that we "get." As we slowly soften ideas of "normalcy" as a goal, for example, we may find greater compassion for ourselves and others in the diversity of human life paths. As we move toward an ecologically sustainable diet, we may find better health, more energy, and longevity. As we let go of our family's or peers' ideas about the trajectory of our careers, we might find new clarity about our true calling. As we try to conform our bodies less to the approval of others, we may learn to love our bodies more, exactly in their own natural state. And as we slowly draw our own lives into greater authenticity, abundance, balance, and integrity, we simultaneously contribute in small ways to transforming the world for all those who come after us. As we progressively decamp from the worship of other gods, life will simply get better... because other gods ultimately, in the words of midrash, "bring no advantage to those who adore them."

But of all the gifts we may "get" in the ongoing practice of the first commandment, perhaps the most delicious is dignity. We begin to live with a kind of gravitas and weightedness, so that we are not blown off our feet by any social or commercial breeze that passes by. We cease giving away our power. As we slow our scrambling for the approval of others, we recognize that we don't really need the material things (or the Facebook "likes") for which we once felt so desperate. As we undertake a sober reordering of priorities in our lives, we can find great spiritual groundedness. We can find a spaciousness and clarity inside of us in which we are proud of who we are and need only YHVH and our communal traditions for guidance. We claim the power, supported by Reality itself, to elevate our own liberation and that of others above all else. In this sense the first commandment is wonderfully circular: we seek the dignity to have no other gods but that which liberates us from other gods.

The First Blessing

The prologue to the Ten Commandments, where YHVH is introduced as the power that brings us out from the land of Egypt, from a house of slaves, promises freedom. But it does not promise that freedom can be attained individually. The exodus from Egypt was a liberation of an entire people all at once from their collective *mitzrayim*. Individual players acted courageously and made sacrifices—Miriam acted bravely and astutely to save her baby brother from murder; Moses stood up to the Pharaoh despite his terror; Nachshone walked headlong into the ocean, legend has it, with the waters reaching his nose before they split and the Israelites escaped. But no single slave could have gotten up on his own, refused to lay one more brick, and left the others in the desert dust. The first commandment is addressed to each of us in the singular, with the understanding that it will only be fully realized, someday, through activating the power of YHVH collectively.

This commandment expresses the radical faith that together, we can make YHVH—the life force and power of liberation—our only God. We can make the health and healing of the earth more important than corporate profits. We can create a culture in which we value work according to the life-affirming good it does, rather than how much profit it makes. We can build a society that values our bodies as they are—where every color, every shape is considered an awesome manifestation of the divine. We can build real relationships with one another, seeing the holiness in each other's eyes, instead of seeing each other's usefulness. In YHVH, the "other" dissolves and we are free to love our neighbors as ourselves.

In this way, the first commandment serves as an

umbrella for the other nine. All the other commandments are practical techniques and spiritual technologies aimed toward realizing this great vision of oneness with the source of life and the dream of liberation. This liberation is for all of us, from the immigrant salon worker who knows she needs it to the subprime mortgage broker who doesn't know he needs it. It's for the healing of our alienation from one another; for the end of the secret nausea that we carry when we do work that exploits others and the earth; for relationships in which each person can be known and recognized and loved for who they are. Some of us—and we know who we are—are more able because of our social position to take risks to this end than others. But all of us have the ability to struggle with our personal other gods and to struggle to break free from our personal *mitzrayim*. With compassion for ourselves and others, we are never required to do something we are unable to do.

As noted in the introduction, the Ten Commandments are not known in Jewish tradition as "ten commandments," but simply as *aseret hadibrot*—"ten things." These are the ten things, the ten words, the ten concepts needed for the transformation of our spirits and our society. To the extent that we have choice, perhaps "you shall have no other gods besides me" functions as a commandment, insisting that we act from the place of YHVH in our hearts—pushing us to act on behalf of the life force of the earth and on behalf of freedom for all its creatures. But to the extent that we don't have choice, to the extent that we ourselves are trapped in the *mitzrayim* of our historical moment, perhaps it is a blessing: May you be free from the painful voices of your past. May you be free from the poverty inflicted by an unjust society. May you be free from the concept of the "other" and free from loneliness. May you be free from all that enslaves you. May you someday come through the opening in the sea to a new life of love and hope on the other side. *May you* have no other gods besides YHVH.

T'MUNAH

▼

The Second Commandment

Do Not Make for Yourself
a Sculpted Image; Do Not
Bow to Them, Do Not
Serve Them

▲

*Accept No Substitutes for
God's Power of Liberation*

Do not make for yourself a sculpted image or any likeness of what is in the skies above, or on the earth below, or in the waters under the earth. Do not bow down to them and do not serve them.

Apparently, downloading text onto stone tablets takes a long time, because while Moses is up on Mount Sinai receiving the Ten Commandments, the people waiting down in the desert below get fed up. They wonder what's taking so long, what Moses is doing up there, and whether he's ever coming back. Come to think of it, they don't know if this God of his is real to begin with. They're starting to lose the thread of what this God had been about—this abstract, formless force of liberation that had taken them out of Egypt. It's hard to hold on to their faith when the miracles aren't happening right then and there. They've heard a big voice, but they've never seen this God. Moses said he had heard a voice coming from a burning bush—but what does that prove? And when Moses had asked the voice to identify itself, it had just replied with evasive obfuscations like,

"I will be what I will be." It's all just too abstract. They decide that they need a *real* God, something shiny and solid that they can see and touch and make sacrifices to—one to whom they can pray for rain.

And so they prevail upon Aaron, Moses' brother, to help. He instructs them to give him all their gold earrings—symbols of prestige and wealth. He melts the jewelry down and casts an idol, a golden calf. In a feat of Orwellian doublethink, they then convince themselves that it was this calf-god, not YHVH, who actually liberated them from slavery. They tell each other, "*This* is your god who brought you out of the land of Egypt!" Aaron builds an altar in front of it and the people pray to it and make burnt offerings. Such idols, especially depictions of a bull, were common objects of worship in the ancient Near East. One in particular was worshipped in Egypt—the Apis bull, representing strength and fertility. This idol that the people now worship, therefore, reeks of Egypt, the site of their former enslavement. In praying to the golden calf, the Israelites are reviving the god of their captors and submitting to it. In so doing, they renounce their own hard-won spiritual liberation.

An even deeper connection lies in the gold itself. This is Egyptian gold (gold from the *mitzrayim*, or place of constriction), which the Israelites managed to finesse out of Egypt during their escape. The jewelry belonged to the Egyptians who had enslaved them and now has been adopted by the Israelites as symbols of their own wealth. Perhaps this gold from the "house of slaves" functions like Superman's kryptonite, a toxic remnant of a former world that spiritually weakens the people to the point of collapse. Perhaps it silently carries with it the molecular structure of enslavement in the service of money. They find themselves bowing down and serving their own status symbols. They replace the God of liberation with the God of materialism and appearances. They renounce the eternal, infinite God in favor of something far simpler, circumscribed, and concrete, which they then imbue with imagined power.

Consecrating an Idol

Idols in the ancient Near East were sculptures of gods in the form of anthropomorphic beings or animals. These images would be brought to life through an elaborate ritual that was thought to draw down the influx of the god energy into the object. Once this ritual was complete, the idol was real; in some cases it would be able to eat and drink the food offerings made and, more importantly, hear and answer prayers. This ritual of transubstantiation was sometimes called a "mouth washing" ritual because it involved washing the mouth of the idol several times. In between each washing there would be ceremonial acts and incantations designed to remove all traces of the human creation of the idol. The tools used to make the sculpture would be thrown into the river and a priest would declare that these tools were the tools of heaven, not of humans. Lastly and most dramatically, the workman who had crafted the sculpture would allow his hands to be bound and then symbolically chopped off with a wooden sword, declaring, "I did not create the statue! I did not create the statue at all! It was [the craftsman god] who created the statue!"

People would then make sacrificial offerings to the idol. These were offerings of something valuable— a grain or fresh produce or a live animal to be killed before the altar. It needed to be something that was expensive, valuable, and truly difficult to part with— a genuine sacrifice. These offerings were thought to appease and please the god. The god would in turn answer prayers, forgive sins, or bring rain and abundant harvest or fertility, depending on the god. This practice had such deep roots in the ancient Near East that the Israelites made sacrifices to YHVH until around 70 CE when the temple was destroyed and there was no longer a physical place to perform the ritual. But Moses and the early rabbinic teachers saw a world of difference between sacrificing to Being and the Source of liberation and sacrificing to idols made by human hands.

As the Exodus story continues, when Moses is about to come back down the mountain to rejoin his people, God breaks the bad news of what the people have been doing in his absence. God is exasperated, hurling insults at the Israelites, calling them "stiff necked" and threatening to destroy them all. Moses pleads successfully on their behalf and then makes his way down the mountain, carrying the two stone tablets of the Ten Commandments. But when he sees the people dancing, praying, and singing around the golden calf, Moses himself becomes so enraged that he smashes the tablets down on the ground and breaks them. "I offered them contact with Being itself! How could they have fallen for this cheap substitute?! How could they have convinced themselves that this hunk of metal that they made from their own earrings has any power?" He is bereft that the people are now worshipping a mere *t'munah*—an image— in lieu of the real thing. At the bottom of the mountain Moses confronts his brother.

Aaron, in a move reminiscent of the tool-throwing and hand-chopping rituals, denies responsibility for having made the idol. He claims that the people gave him their gold, he hurled it into the fire, and "out came this calf!" He vouches for the power of the idol in order to cover his own embarrassing complicity in the act. Eventually Moses goes back up the mountain for a replacement set of commandments.

In a sense, the whole story seems so far-fetched, it's a wonder that the prohibition on idol worship was included in the Ten Commandments to begin with. In editing a list of the top ten rules for spiritual and ethical living, one might think it would be unnecessary to prohibit people from worshipping their own jewelry. One might think it would be unnecessary to prohibit someone from making a sculpture and then falsely claiming that he had merely thrown some metal into a fire and a live animal-god had popped out all by itself. All of this sounds a bit ridiculous to contemporary ears. These kinds of things could only be imagined in ancient times. We in enlightened modernity would never be so foolish. Would we?

Idols and Brands

Every month about 43,000 men go out and buy a Chevrolet Silverado pickup truck. They buy it despite the fact that it's expensive, gets poor gas mileage, can't seat many people, and despite the fact that the Car Talk guys, when they were on the air, used to say, "Unless you are *picking something up*, a pickup truck is a ludicrous car to drive!"

Most of these guys are not picking anything up except, they hope, a date. Here's how the Silverado is marketed: "THE NEW FACE OF STRONG. Strength. Reliability. The new Silverado pairs brains with brawn to build upon the legacy of the most dependable, longest-lasting full-size pickup trucks on the road." Who can blame these men for wanting this? What man isn't raised to want to be strong, reliable, have brains and brawn, and to be long lasting and full size? This is the essence of the traditional ideal of masculinity and it is an ineffable, elusive quality of the spirit. Sometimes men want this so badly, they buy an impractical, expensive object in hopes that in an almost magical way, they'll be able to access and embody that spiritual power through the object.

Facial products are marketed to women in parallel ways. When Moses came down from Mount Sinai carrying the tablets of the Ten Commandments, it is said that his face was glowing—radiant from his contact with God. He had to hide his face under a veil so as not to scare people. But thanks to the Industrial Revolution, we don't have to commune with God to get that glow. We can use what are called "luminizing" beauty products like Amazonian Clay BB Illuminating Moisturizer, Avène Timeless Radiance, Skin Illuminator in Peach, or Liquid Luster in Gold. There are hundreds of products that will give us the glow of spiritual inner light on our faces. Or if we're hurting and lonely, Sephora has a product called "Nurture Me" with the tagline, "soothing crème cushions skin with nourishing vitamins." With this cream, we can be soothed and cushioned and nourished—nurtured like a mother would nurture us. In her classic feminist work *The Beauty Myth*, Naomi Wolf lays out exactly how spiritual light is projected into the brands of these products. These products promise direct contact with some form of the divine. And so we buy them.

These are modern forms of idol worship. We make a sacrificial offering of money to an object that we believe will grant us special powers, good fortune, fertility (i.e., sex appeal), or abundance. The more we pay and the more it hurts to make the sacrifice, the more of these intangible powers we feel we are buying. Of course it's not literally the object itself that carries the power; it's the brand. The brand of our consumer products plays the role of the god that animates the idol. Anyone who really thinks about it knows that a high-top shoe will not transform one's life, but the shoe comes infused with power and meaning, and so we believe it will. We buy different brands at different times throughout our days and years because each one offers different powers and rules over different jurisdictions, just like the gods of old. Apple offers us one set of powers, Coca-Cola another, and Under Armour yet another.

The Brand as the Platonic Form

The power of the brand goes well beyond the product itself. On pretty much any street corner in New York you can buy one of those knockoff Coach handbags. Everyone knows they're not the real thing. And just the fact that they're sitting there in the open air for $12.99 seems to tarnish the brand. But people buy them. Because the shimmering ideal represented by the Coach brand isn't found on the shelves of Saks Fifth Avenue either. No *actual* bag, no matter how expensive, no matter how beautifully lit from above and below, fully captures it. The brand lives on a plane all of its own, forever unattainable.

The brand is a Platonic form. Plato's theory of forms says that everything in the real world has a corresponding ideal version in the world of ideas. This "ideal" version is called the "form." So a handbag is a particular example of the general idea or form of Handbag with a capital *H*. And to Plato, the form is primary; everything in our world is just a flawed, derivative knockoff. Things in this world change, they come, they go. The form is eternal and unchanging. There's love as we know it between people in our world and then there's "Platonic Love"—Plato's pure ideal, unsullied with real life.

To the extent that our engagement with a brand gives us even glancing access to a Platonic form, that engagement goes beyond the purely transactional—the experience of shopping and buying is worshipful. People flock to a new product release like it's a religious service with awe in their eyes, waiting in line for hours to be the first ones in the door. Temples in the big cities feature oversized renditions of the product, lit up and sparkling and festooned like an ancient idol. But smaller, everyday products too, like McDonald's Big Macs and Gillette razors, have that subtle sheen of greatness. We get not only the calories and the clean shave, but a brick in the edifice of our identity and a sense of being part of something larger than ourselves. We make our sacrifice and we receive something that we feel we can't obtain any other way. And so each purchase becomes a small act of supplication.

Does it work? Yes and no. There can certainly be a placebo effect when we buy a new pair of Nike running shoes or a Samsung device. We may feel stronger, smarter, or more happily embedded in the subculture of our choosing. We may feel more beautiful wearing a new dress, edgier after buying an Urban Outfitters messenger bag, or more manly after buying a Harley. The sense of spiritual power that we've imbibed through the brand/god and the ritual act of purchasing the product may stay with us for a while. It may actually have a positive impact on our lives in the way that greater confidence often does. But eventually the luster fades because, of course, the product doesn't have real power any more than the idol statue does. Some products are useful and they help us do our work and live our lives, but none of them go beyond that, as promised by the brand, and fundamentally transform us as people. A man driving a Chevrolet Silverado is still the same man and a woman wearing Liquid Luster in Gold is still the same woman. As the product ages—and this can happen very quickly, depending on the product—its life force dims and the Platonic form recedes into the ether.

Serving Our Own Creations

The symbolism of the golden calf episode is not subtle: instead of worshipping the real God—*Being* itself and the power of liberation—the people begin to worship symbols of their own status and wealth. They worship a *t'munah*. (This is exactly the kind of "other god" whose worship is prohibited by the first commandment.) The second commandment gets more granular in specifying that it is the *manufacture* and worship of a *t'munah* that is at issue. A key to understanding this text is the Hebrew word *lecha*—"for yourself." The text says, "Do not make *for yourself* a sculpted image...Do not bow down to them and do not serve them." So a violation of this commandment has to include two parts: (1) we have to make a sculpted image somehow in our own self-interest and then (2) we have to elevate the object and give up our power to it. In the capitalist economy, the people doing the making and the people doing the supplication are not necessarily the same people. The first half of the commandment addresses us in our capacity as producers of objects; the second half addresses us in our capacity as consumers. But the whole system thrives on collective violations of this commandment.

Those who own the means of production "sculpt" the object. They do this by hiring low-wage workers to physically make it and high-wage workers to give it its brand power. Then the two processes are very carefully cleaved from one another. The production process is erased from public view in the same way that the production of an idol is erased by the mouth-washing ritual. By the time it reaches the store shelf, a pair of Gap jeans cannot show the fingerprints of the sweatshop laborers who stitched them or the traces of the pesticides used to grow the cotton. It can't reveal the hundreds of middle managers guiding its distribution or the lawyers toiling away on obscure aspects of commercial law. It can't betray the market research and hundreds of focus groups that went into engineering the style and look and feel. It must be reborn as a magical garment infused with spiritual power, ready to transmit that power to the faithful. Companies go to great lengths to render the production process invisible. The mouth of the product is washed so that it cannot speak of where it came from. Like the idol, the consumer product must seem as if it wasn't *made*, but simply *is*.

Through our consumer practices we "bow down to" and "serve" idols. At its most extreme, our worship takes the form of buying things that we really cannot afford, prioritizing the acquisition of the product and the brand power over our financial and physical well-being. But even those of us who shop within our means are often choosing to buy products that we don't need over facilitating longer-term life goals, saving for retirement, giving more to charity, or investing in organizations that are doing good in the world. Virtually all middle-class and wealthy Americans do this. None of us could justify this behavior from an ethical standpoint if pressed, and yet it is normal and accepted in our culture. We are encouraged to give some money to charity and keep most "for ourselves," meaning keep it to buy products that we don't need in the mistaken belief that they will infuse us with powers that we *do* need. Because our culture supports the notion that products carry these powers, the expenditure of our hard-earned money on them is considered justifiable. The money that we spend on consumer goods is a form of tribute to the gods we believe can be invoked through those goods.

A "Need" for Barbie Hello Dreamhouse

Beyond the actual dollars we spend as tribute is the attitude we bring to the ritual. We hear every year or so of shoppers trampled at Walmart or Target by mobs desperate to buy a new toaster or sweater. Dozens of people will camp overnight outside an Apple store to be the first to buy the new generation of iPhone. Others will wait in line for hours to get a photo autographed by a media star. On a more regular basis, when people talk about their desire for new products, they speak in the language of "need." Someone who owns a useable pair of shoes will say, "I need new shoes." A parent looking for a holiday gift for his daughter will say, "I need to get a Barbie Hello Dreamhouse." Buying new and popular things seems almost compulsory in our culture. To fail to supply them to our children can feel like cruel deprivation; to fail to attain them for ourselves can threaten our sense of normalcy.

Since the only culturally plausible reason for not buying a desired product is that one can't afford it (the notion of thrift as a virtue is largely outmoded), such products also serve as a marker of class. We buy the products that others in our class buy and so safeguard our class status. This principle applies to other aspects of our social identity as well—race, ethnicity, generation, hometown, and political and religious affiliation. Each subgroup has its own uniform of clothing and goods we buy to cement our place in it. Within the range of the uniform, if we can afford it, we then choose products to express our individual "personality." (Each person is thought to be as unique as a snowflake and yet that uniqueness is somehow best expressed through products marketed to the masses.) Our purchases play a vital role in constructing who we are. As marketing guru Seth Godin puts it, when we buy a product, we are buying the opportunity "to join a group that matters."

In the subtlest form of supplication to our idols, we simply pay a great deal of attention to them. Buying, having, and using products of all kinds, well beyond what we actually need, is at the heart of American culture. We talk about products frequently, as if they are inherently important and as if our ability to get them or not get them will have grave consequences. There is a reason why we use the term "*paying* attention": when we give our attention to something, we are allocating a precious resource to it—in this case, our focus and time. We are giving it power and gravitas. We are simultaneously taking that attention, that mental and emotional energy, away from something else. Our attention is a kind of payment.

Capitalism depends upon the collective, ongoing two-part violations of the second commandment. Part one: corporations make objects that, through their brands, form the image of some spiritual or psychological quality, packed with meaning and power. They become a *t'munah* of something greater. Part two: consumers pursue and buy these objects with varying degrees of need, fervor, and obsequiousness.

We yield our power to branded objects with sacrifices of time, attention, and money. We feel we need them to live the lives we want and be the people we want to be, as if products have magical powers and can answer to our prayers. Our faith in these things—created by other humans and human organizations that generally have no interest in our well-being—is affirmed by a culture of commerce. We become ensnared, losing sight of YHVH up the mountain, and we forget that from the beginning these shiny objects were just our own jewelry—imported from the *house of slaves*—melted down and reshaped and repackaged for our consumption. We look helplessly to brands for salvation.

Simulations

The second commandment prohibits making "a sculpted image or any likeness," not just of God, but of anything in the skies, earth, or water—that is, anything at all. This would seem to rule out not only making idols, but making any representational art. Clearly this is not how generations of Jewish and Christian artists have interpreted this commandment. A gentler interpretation is that this commandment prohibits the making of simulations. It prohibits making a fake version of something real, especially *lecha*, for yourself, for your own benefit or profit. Even worse is doing what the Israelites did with the golden calf—making such a thing for your own profit and then trying to convince yourself or others that it is, in fact, real.

Genetically modified organisms (GMOs) are a prime example of such a simulation of a living thing found in the skies, earth, or water. A company like Monsanto will engineer a new kind of corn, wheat, tomato, or fish that looks and tastes similar to a naturally growing variety. The corporation makes this sculpted image "for itself." The GMO enriches the company immensely because it creates its own market of farmers and customers who previously had no need for it. It usually either allows farmers to drench their land in herbicides and pesticides to which the GMO crop alone is impervious but which kill everything else in the area (with disastrous environmental and human consequences) or to buy seeds that grow into sterile plants, forcing them to buy new seeds every year (also with disastrous environmental and human consequences, especially in the developing world).

The GMO manufacturer then strives to conceal the simulation from consumers—to pass off a GMO tomato as a natural tomato, hence the GMO labeling controversy. Corporations like Monsanto are spending millions in legal battles to gain the right to engage in the corporate equivalent of the mouth-washing ritual—erasing the human origins of the product (that it was made by scientists in a lab) and passing it off as nature's or God's creation. Corporate-produced simulations are a staple of commercial strategy. The second commandment stands against that strategy, exhorting us, as producers, to be honest about our products and, as consumers, to never choose a simulation over the real thing.

In noncommercial matters, we often mistake simulations for the real thing. We mistake social prestige for personal power; we mistake superficial attractiveness for inner beauty; we mistake competitive games for moral battles; we mistake thinness for health; we mistake money for wealth. We imbue the temporal with the significance of the eternal. We worship the finite as if it were the infinite. It's no coincidence that the word "idol" means both an image of a human in the form of a movie star and an image of a god in the form of a golden calf.

Sculpting Our Own Images

The most personal and private way in which we violate the second commandment is not in sculpting physical images in the form of products, but in sculpting our own images. Perhaps "Do not make for yourself a sculpted image" could be reread as, "Do not sculpt your image. Do not make of yourself a simulation." We sculpt our own bodies, first and foremost, to project an image that is not our own. We turn ourselves into simulations. When someone goes to the tanning salon, they are making themselves a simulation of someone who has been spending time in the sun. When someone lifts weights to build up their muscles, they are making themselves a simulation of someone who uses their body for labor and play. When someone colors their hair, they are making themselves a simulation of someone with different-colored hair or someone younger. And when someone clothes themselves in an Armani suit, H&M leggings, or a Metallica T-shirt that says, "Ride the Lightning," they are making themselves a simulation of someone who embodies the myth of each of those brands.

Beyond our physical appearance, we sometimes sculpt our online personas, carefully curating the photos, the types of information and posts we share, trying to match the personal brand of those with social cachet. Some of us even adjust our speaking style, often without even realizing it, mimicking the style of TV or film characters, belligerent talk show hosts, or the dulcet tones of National Public Radio reporters.

Of graver import, many of us shape our careers or decisions about family based on other people, real or archetypal, whom we think we ought to emulate. Someone may decide to work a particular job or to have children, not because they feel called to do so, but because working that job or having children conforms to the sculpted shape of a life deemed successful by society. We make walking, talking topiaries of ourselves. We invest so much energy forming ourselves into the likeness of others that sometimes we don't know who we really are.

The Optics

Sometime after the golden calf incident, God tells Moses,

> Okay, here's what we're gonna do: Tell the people to build a house for me . . . sure, with fabulous

gold and royal draperies, go ahead. Make it complex inside, with concentric layers and inner chambers. (Now, you know and I know that I don't need a "house," but they seem to really need a place to *go* to connect with me.) And tell them to perform sacrifices and burn incense and say specific prayers. (You know and I know that I don't really care about rituals but they seem to really need something to *do* to connect with me.) And tell them to place in the innermost chamber two cherubim, like angels, facing each other. Tell them that in the space between these two cherubim, that is where my spirit will dwell. (You know and I know that I am everywhere, but at least this way, if we say that I'm in that negative space between two things, they might not be so tempted to reduce me to a thing.)

The people build this moveable temple in the desert. Imagine it as a Wi-Fi hot spot to connect with God. In the temple is the Ark of the Covenant, a chest containing the two stone tablets of the Ten Commandments. Later when the moveable, tentlike temple is replaced by the palatial stone temple in Jerusalem, the Ark of the Covenant sits in the center.

Here the biblical narrative blends into history: the

Ark, the tablets, and the temple itself become idols. The people can't grasp the concept that all of this flamboyant symbolism is just a way to focus their spiritual energies on God. People come to worship the things rather than the God of liberation. They come to worship the place rather than the power of Spirit. Jerusalem becomes the site of conflicts, pain, and war, which continues to this day. Such is the danger of trying to represent and locate God.

What a world of trouble we've gotten ourselves into by worshipping things! Material wealth and appearances are optical illusions. We're never going to find true happiness, real relationships, or a deep connection with the living, loving God if we don't let go of our idols. And unfortunately many of us don't find this out until the end of our lives.

The canon of urban mythology is brimming with stories of people on their deathbeds looking back on their lives with some form of regret. They wish they had spent less time pursuing wealth, beauty, prestige, and power and more time with their families, more time with God, more time with themselves. They wish they had not bowed down and served the wrong priorities.

Occasionally we hear of people who get a second chance—who are given a terminal diagnosis that turns out to be wrong or who have a fatal accident from which they are resuscitated. When they are released from their hospital room and go back into the world, they plunge into real life for the first time with abandon, authenticity, vigor, and gratitude. They invariably see their near-death experience as the greatest blessing of their lives, because now they are free to really live. One man who barely emerged from a coma after a car accident tearfully told his family to bear no grudge against the driver at fault, explaining, "Because of him I got to shake the hand of God." People like this man no longer care about the stuff they have; they no longer care about projecting an enhanced image of themselves; they no longer care about the optics.

Keeping It Real

Rabbi Zalman Schachter-Shalomi, the founder of a modern mystical movement in Judaism, says that when you think about dying and having to account for your life, you shouldn't worry that God will ask, "Why were you not more like Moses? Why were you not more like Sarah or Rachel?" You should worry that God will ask, "Why were you not more like you?" He understands that the commandment to not worship something fake is really a commandment to not *be* something fake.

We squander so much of our own life force trying

to become something other than what we are. We try so hard to achieve in so many arenas—to have the right kind of body, the right kind of job, the right kind of friends, the right kind of online persona, the right kind of family, the right kind of kids in the right kind of neighborhood. Whether it is a suburban home in Schaumburg, Illinois, where you can park the SUV in the driveway or a brownstone in Williamsburg, Brooklyn, where you can sport tattoos and an ironic mustache, we pursue what feels satisfying and fun and do what we feel we have to do to be loved. We're starving for social validation, and like the Israelites who made the golden calf, we get impatient waiting for the few-and-far-between flashes of revelation that return us to our real selves.

The second commandment challenges us to keep it real—to be real about who we are and to be real about who God is. We really *are* unique and beautiful as snowflakes and we require no adornment. All the true power that we have in this world comes from our connection to our most authentic selves, sometimes called our God-selves. The more "like ourselves" we are, the deeper our experience of life and relationships. It is the height of personal liberation when we can accept no substitutes and no simulations. We do not need to worship the *t'munah*. Real life, unfiltered by brands, is spectacular. Real humans, unmediated by products, are wondrous.

LASHAV

▼

The Third Commandment

Do Not Take the Name of God in Vain

▲

Defend the Goodness of God; Take Responsibility for Resistance and Change

Do not take the name of YHVH, your God, in vain; for YHVH will not acquit one who takes YHVH's name in vain.

Controlling how reality is characterized is powerful politics. One of the shrewdest tricks of those who would pass oppressive laws and inhibit change is to brand the world as a terrible place. The worse things are, the more justified is an attitude of fear, an embattled stance of aggression toward the other, and a scrambling for resources deemed scarce.

If voter fraud is rampant and millions of people are voting illegally, it becomes reasonable to establish stringent voting requirements. (When this disenfranchises certain people, well, that's just the cost of preventing malfeasance.)

If we are all in imminent danger of being massacred by Islamic terrorists, it becomes essential to keep Muslims out of the country and cast a suspicious eye on those already here. (When this denies the humanity of Muslims and endangers and isolates them, well, that's just the cost of public safety.)

Whoever controls the tenor and tone of how our world is represented controls our social landscape and our religious discourse. Nothing could be more fundamental to our experience of life and our choices, our politics, and our faith than our beliefs about the nature of reality.

The prohibition against taking the name of God in vain is perhaps the subtlest and most profound of the commandments because it addresses this question of how reality is characterized. While this commandment is commonly thought to refer only to God's name, remember that the name YHVH is not actually a name; it's a form of the verb "to be," like "I am becoming" or simply "I am." YHVH signifies the ground of being itself. It's the biggest word in the world. YHVH contains the entire universe of possibility—the little that we know and the vast expanse that we don't know. YHVH includes the world of supermarkets and cars, people with guns, nursing mothers, melting glaciers, and social media. YHVH is reality as a whole.

When this commandment prohibits taking YHVH's name in vain or falsely, it is protecting the narrative of "how things are"—the way the *real world* is described—from defamation. We could rewrite the commandment in this way: do not misrepresent reality.

The Fall from Innocence

Our world does have dangers. People are sometimes selfish, sometimes violent, and sometimes dishonest. But the notion of the world as fundamentally hostile and dangerous has become foundational to our society and needs to be questioned. It preys on our fears: life is cast as so perilous and humans as so depraved that we need to shelter ourselves within systems of barricades and hierarchies. Free market capitalism is predicated on the notion that people will always (and only) act in their own financial self-interest. Our criminal justice system is structured to punish and deter lawbreakers. Our laws protect property from the encroachments of others. Optimists and "innocents" are advised that if they know what's good for them, they will adopt a healthy dose of cynicism and fall from innocence quickly.

The "fall from innocence," as defined by one online commentator, is "when you realize the world is cruel and harsh." This realization is assumed to dawn on every child, ideally slowly but sometimes suddenly, and it is cast as a healthy and natural rite of passage in our culture. The fall from innocence concept is assumed to be ideologically neutral in that it simply describes a mature response to a world that *is*, in fact, cruel and harsh. Part of the charm of younger children, we say, is that they haven't figured this out yet—they still walk around expecting the world to be fair, strangers to be nice, and skies to be sunny. We love that about children. We love to wax poetic about them and their intact innocence.

But transpose those same qualities onto an adult, and he or she is no longer so adorable. Such a person is labeled "naïve" and "a sucker" (the alt-right term is a "cuck"), easy prey for human predators. Such a person is seen as not fully adult. Cruelty and harshness in our world are a given. Fundamental selfishness is a given. The Darwinian competitive nature of life is a given. We are imagined to be seated across from, not next to, our neighbor. We are fundamentally alone. Transitioning to adulthood entails recognizing all of this, balancing it with cautious doses of positive thinking to stave off despair, and preparing to live life accordingly. To become guarded is a fundamental part of what it means to grow up in America.

This vision of life that includes a healthy fall from innocence is assumed to be apolitical and areligious. It's thought to be simply an honest, unvarnished appraisal of reality. But often the most dangerous discourses are the ones that position themselves as not political or religious, but merely as common sense, obvious truth, or simple practicality. Folk wisdom can be treacherous.

It has led to discrimination against women, people of color, and gays and lesbians over the centuries, for example, by falsely imputing essential characteristics to them. Similarly, the model of a "cruel and harsh" world feeds an ideology that is deeply political and theologically dishonest. It presents a very particular narrative of "the way things are."

Defaming God

In popular culture, the third commandment is about yelling "Jesus Christ!" when you stub your toe. We picture nuns rapping their students on the knuckles for the sin of swearing. This is clearly not the intention of the text, yet there is an implication here about reserving God language for when we really mean it. We are called to recognize the power of language in this teaching. What we say matters; how we say it matters; and it matters whether it's true, particularly when it comes to talking about God and ultimate reality.

The word "take" in this commandment is a translation of the Hebrew verb *tisa*. A better translation may be "pick up and carry off." *Tisa* was used in transactions in the ancient Near East to indicate the sealing of a deal. When someone would buy something and pay for it, it was the moment that the customer *nasa*

(past tense of *tisa*)—picked it up and carried it away—
that the deal was final. It connoted ownership. This
commandment conveys picking up and carrying away
God's name, claiming ownership, appropriating it. The
commandment does not prohibit use of God's name,
only using the name "in vain." The Hebrew word is
lashav, which means "without meaning" or "for empti-
ness" or "falsely"—outside a proper meaning, common
or unimportant, or without the sanctity that should
be there.

In his beautiful series on Jewish ethics, Rabbi Joseph
Telushkin points out that the third commandment was
violated routinely by the nineteenth-century Southern-
ers who justified slavery by saying that it was approved
of in the Bible and by God. To say that the Bible
approves of slavery is a manipulation of the truth that
the Bible does not explicitly allow or disallow slavery—it
acknowledges slavery. Biblical laws protecting the rights
of slaves did not exist in the American South. For example, while biblical law forbids forcibly returning a slave
who has run away, this was the practice in the United
States and was ruled legal with the *Dred Scott* decision
in 1857. The falsehood that the Bible condoned slavery
was used to great effect. God and the biblical tradition
were falsely linked with something evil.

In biblical tradition, *this*—the appropriation of

God and the Bible to justify immorality—is considered indefensible. The second half of the commandment to not take God's name in vain says, "for YHVH will not acquit one who takes YHVH's name in vain." This is not said about murder. The Ten Commandments do not make killing, stealing, or committing adultery offenses without acquittal. Violating this particular commandment is singularly abhorrent, as though this is the one that God takes personally. Violations of any of the other commandments merely reflect badly on the human who did it. This one, when violated, reflects badly on God. This third commandment is about God's reputation. This one imputes sins to God—sins of which God is innocent.

Who Cares about God's Reputation?

So then the question becomes, so what? So what if God's reputation as a good and loving and just God gets tarnished? What happens then? Why should God care? Why should we care?

What happens is, *people lose faith*. Faith gets injured when public figures use the concept of God opportunistically to justify evil acts. Faith can collapse when religious institutions or representatives of God act badly themselves. Extreme examples of this abound.

Queer people, and often those who care about them, have become alienated from religious life because of clergy brandishing questionable biblically based claims about the sinfulness of their relationships and genders. Muslims describe fleeing Islam because of the association with terrorism in God's name. Jewish women have recoiled from the persistent image of an angry, patriarchal God and religious texts plastered with masculine pronouns. The Catholic Church hemorrhaged members due to the child sex abuse scandals. That the abuse was so pervasive and systematically concealed was soul crushing to Catholics around the world.

The losses sustained when *people lose faith* are painful, even traumatic. In most cases of the defamation of God's character, the believer is alienated not just from the religious institution, but from God. Our notions of God are interwoven with the people who speak about God and institutions that teach about God. When reality is misrepresented, when God's reputation as a good and loving God gets tarnished, it's hard to disentangle this from our own beliefs. We lose faith, and faith, once lost, is difficult to retrieve.

Atheist and humanist movements have benefitted tremendously from violations of the third commandment. Today, the group of people who describe themselves as religiously "nothing in particular" or "spiritual but not religious" is second in number only to Christians. Most of these people were born into a religious tradition and left. Many were alienated from their faith and their birth religions when they were told that, for example, their favorite uncle was going to hell because he had not accepted Jesus Christ as his lord and savior. Many of them were exposed to institutions and leaders that pinned on God their own bigotry and small-mindedness. This exposure was toxic. It was toxic to their faith and to their lives in general. They left religion often painfully disillusioned. Even years later, they can be deeply suspicious of God or anything that sounds too "religious."

But mainstream and conservative religion has continued to perpetuate an image of God as angry, jealous, and male and condoned the structures of wealth and power that we humans have built to the benefit of the few and the detriment of the many. They have cast God as a punishing and conditionally loving father. They have used "His" name as cover for their own prejudices. They have used the sparkly sanctity of the word "God" to consolidate their own power and to disempower others. Such religious institutions have failed to keep the third commandment and they have failed their own people.

To counter such regressive and dim depictions of

God, progressive theological movements over the last hundred years have developed nuanced interpretations of their traditions, embracing the divine feminine, universal salvation, radical inclusivity, ecological and earth-centered spirituality, and liberation theology in which God stands with the oppressed in fighting for justice. The clergy and theologians of these movements have sifted through their scriptures and pursued their own mystical journeys to recover the loving voice of God. They let go the human intolerance and parochial thinking that so often came bundled with their traditions. In so doing, they have honored God's name and embraced the spirit of the third commandment. Those lucky enough to discover these movements often feel blessed beyond measure to have found a way back to faith.

Defaming Reality

Whenever we sigh in resignation over something we dislike and say, "Well, that's just the way it is," the *it* to which we're referring is the ground of being: existence, life, nature, human nature, reality. We throw up our hands and say, "Boys will be boys." "There will always be war." "People will always act in their own economic self-interest." We claim that we have to lie and cheat because that's the way the world is. We project our own prejudices, saying that's just the way the world is. We assume that there will always be economic inequality because that's the way the world is. The philosophy of the "is-ness" of the world gets elucidated through casual speech.

But is the world *really* like that—and can we really know that for sure—or are we opportunistically appropriating this concept of how the world is in order to justify our actions?

The gun rights lobby in the United States prospers under violations of the third commandment: They claim that it's nature, human nature, to be violent. There will always be people who want to shoot up a school or outdoor concert or nightclub and will find some way to do it. So it's best to be *realistic* (meaning "of or related to reality") and arm everyone...so folks can fight back...because that's just how reality is. This lobby can still exist post–Sandy Hook and post–Las Vegas only because of the broader "cruel and harsh world" narrative. It presupposes a world in which people are inherently violent and fundamentally situated in opposition to each other—and a world in which force is the only viable means of effecting change. This defames the character of reality: taking the name of reality in vain, misrepresenting it, appropriating it for one's own purposes, and ruining its reputation.

The climate change denial movement similarly benefits from calculated defamations of reality: When asked about the scientific consensus on human-caused climate change, the denier will say, "The climate is changing because the climate has always been changing. That's just the way it is. There is no law we can pass in Washington that's going to change the weather. The melting of the glaciers, the extinction of plant and animal species, the mass displacement of humans in coastal communities and islands, the droughts, crop failures, and increasingly severe storms around the world are simply the way reality is. Don't blame us; blame life; blame God. The impending suffering is inevitable and the best we can do is try to make sure that it doesn't happen to us. Make sure we've got air-conditioning for when the summers get hot, make sure corporations get first dibs on water as the lakes and rivers dwindle, and make sure our borders are tight for when the climate refugees arrive. It's a cruel and harsh world."

Faith in Life

This narrative too is a violation of the third commandment. It takes the name of YHVH—the concept of reality—and maligns it in order to justify human wrongdoing. And what happens when you do this?

Why should we care? What happens when the massacre of children is not enough to get any significant movement on gun control? What happens when we are told that guns are necessary to defend ourselves in an inherently violent world? What happens when we're told that humans cannot affect the fate of the earth? What happens when we are told that corporations will never become responsible stewards of the environment because executives are always going to make money first and foremost? What happens? *People lose faith.* We lose faith that anything can ever change; we lose faith in the world as a good and beautiful place; we lose faith in each other. We come to feel unsafe, unable to be embraced by the universe. Or maybe, because this kind of libel against life is so commonplace, we never had the chance to gain faith to begin with. We are forced to foreclose on the possibility of change.

In this way the religious right and the political right are the perfect bedfellows. Conservative theology teaches that human nature is befouled by original sin and the *yetzer hara* (the evil inclination). It teaches that God vanquishes enemies and punishes sinners. It teaches that the natural order is beyond human influence and that the embattled social order must resist the rising tide of human chaos. Conservative theologians misrepresent reality and take the name of YHVH in vain, and conservative political ideology floats on the sea of this distorted theology. It offers a parallel world of human dominance and submission, exploitation of the earth, repression of difference, punishment as social control, and war as foreign policy. True peace and justice are pipe dreams and childlike fantasies, not available in this world. Accordingly, the fall from innocence is not only maturity, but sanity. The best we can do is to cut our losses, protect our own, and await the afterlife.

But Wait—*Isn't* the World Cruel and Harsh?

One billion children worldwide are living in poverty. Hundreds of millions worldwide do not have enough food to eat and lack adequate access to clean drinking water. In the United States people of color suffer mass incarceration and one in five women can expect to be sexually assaulted. Rates of depression, drug abuse, eating disorders, and suicides are soaring. *Isn't* the world cruel and harsh? And to the extent that anyone believes that God is in charge, isn't God therefore also cruel and harsh or, at best, indifferent to the cruel, harsh world?

The answer to the question hinges on whether or not poverty, violence, and injustice are built into the structure of reality. Does God make it happen? Is it inevitable? Is all this suffering simply the way *it*—YHVH—is?

The biblical tradition, certainly as seen through the lens of the Creation story, the Exodus story, and the Ten Commandments, says no.

The deep structure of the universe, the default state, the factory settings are inherently good. The Creation story unfolds with a series of spoken creative acts. And at the end of each day, the newly created elements are declared good. The light is good, the water and skies are good, the earth and plants are good, the fish and birds are good, the land animals are good, and the human earthlings along with everything else are deemed *very* good. From an undifferentiated, formless, and void watery darkness, each day the world gets more and more articulated, rich, detailed, and alive. Each step in the process, each evolution, is embraced by the divine. Each new manifestation is loved and accepted. Nothing is rejected; nothing is cast out of the budding universe. This love, this acceptance, even a kind of giddy joy at the dawn of the Technicolor universe is the living heart of the Creation story.

Does the "Fall" of Adam and Eve in Genesis 3 immediately override this inherent goodness? Some Christian traditions teach that it does—that their sin has been transmitted through the generations by a kind of epigenetic inheritance and has tainted us all. Indeed, we do share impulse control issues with the mythical first humans. They ate the forbidden fruit out of childlike curiosity and defiance of authority. But this was part of a natural growth process by which humans test boundaries and gain adult knowledge. There was no malice involved in the act. Adam and Eve represent the childhood of humanity and they suffered what some parents call "natural consequences." They grew up. They became sexual beings, resulting in childbearing, with all the accompanying pain and vulnerability. Instead of being handed food like small children, they henceforth had to provide for themselves through hard work. We have inherited, if anything, a marbled and complex psyche and a propensity to wrestle with God.

It's Us

In the story of the Exodus from Egypt, YHVH is the force of liberation, empowering the Israelites to escape their enslavement. The villains of the story are human actors—the Pharaoh and the Egyptian army are responsible for the oppression and suffering of the Israelites. Their obsession with power and wealth deafens them to the cries of the people and the consequences of their actions. It is their actions that bring down the influx of natural disasters in the form of the ten plagues. Much like the plague of climate change today, the plagues of the Torah were directly tied to human arrogance, greed, and exploitation. The third commandment cautions us: Do not pin the suffering of the Israelites or the suffering of innocent Egyptians, for that matter, on God. Pin it where it belongs: on the wrongdoing of those in power. Do not use the name of YHVH falsely.

Some natural disasters are truly natural, psychiatric conditions can be genetic, and diseases emerge through the indifferent processes of pathogens. But the physical and emotional and spiritual suffering on the scale that we see today is largely caused by human action, not nature, genetics, or evolutionary destiny. And much of the suffering could be alleviated by humans who generally choose not to alleviate it.

Oxfam estimates that to end extreme global poverty—feed the one billion children worldwide who are living in poverty—would take less than one quarter of the total income of the world's top 100 billionaires.

Scientific consensus on global warming, with all its attendant disasters, is that its cause is humans—specifically the consumer and lifestyle practices of people in the developed world.

Refugees perish in the Sonoran Desert and others wash up dead on the shores of Greece because wealthy nations refuse to take them.

Full-time workers languish in poverty and cannot

afford health care for their children because corporations refuse to pay a living wage.

The most deadly ailments of our time, including cancer and heart disease, are exploding due to our diets and exposure to commercial toxins.

The list could go on and on. We humans are doing these things to ourselves. It's us. It's not God. It's not just the way of the world; it is the way we have let the world become. The third commandment does not ask us to naïvely, innocently turn a blind eye to the suffering of our world. The third commandment asks us to properly identify the perpetrator.

Identifying the perpetrator requires the practice of clarification and separation. A world of difference exists between noting that injustice exists and claiming that injustice is the nature of existence. This emphasis on careful separation of concepts and clear delineations is primary in Jewish tradition generally. We are taught to separate meat and dairy, separate Sabbath from the workweek, and separate childhood from adulthood. The first prayer Jews say in the morning is, "Blessed are you, YHVH, our God, who gives me the wisdom to distinguish between day and night." Keeping the third commandment calls us to another such practice of discernment—distinguishing between that which is the nature of YHVH (and therefore unchangeable) and that which is a product of human cultures and systems (and therefore changeable).

The Ten Commandments as well as the other 603 commandments of the Hebrew Bible testify that humanity's fate is in human hands. We are taught how to live, because it matters what we do.

We can imitate the goodness of YHVH, care for one another, fulfill the promise of liberation, and honor the blessings of our ecosystems—the Garden of Eden that we've been given. Or, we can perpetrate injustice and bring plagues upon ourselves. It's our choice. But what the third commandment prohibits us from doing in response to the suffering in the world is to throw up our hands and say, "Well, that's just the way things are." That is misrepresenting God, using the name of YHVH falsely. We are called to take responsibility for what we and our human cultures have created. And where God and reality are innocent, we are required to refrain from libel.

The Countercultural Vision of the Third Commandment

Taking or using the name of YHVH in vain—*lashav*— happens not only in our own minds, but in the ways that we represent reality in public. The third commandment is ultimately about speech acts. It acknowledges the power of speech, spoken and written, to transform the world. In this way, it links again to the Creation story (Genesis 1–3). In this story, God speaks the world into existence. Each new cosmic and earthly creation is formed through speech alone. "God said, 'Let there be light.' And there was light." There is no separate creative act that mediates between the speech and the creation—the speech itself brings something new into existence. Speech is generative.

We have seen how speech that violates this commandment can generate hatred and fear. Such violations have been used to great effect by the religious right to control the narrative about religion and by the political right to control the narrative about reality. The cruel-and-harsh-world narrative is dominant in our society and has shaped much of public policy, foreign policy, environmental policy, and our social landscapes. By promulgating the image of an angry, jealous, male God who hates gays and wants women subservient, the religious right has successfully pried progressives away from religion. Accepting this characterization of God and religion, progressives have ceded territory and yielded power, reach, and moral authority to conservative forces.

To keep the third commandment is to reclaim this

territory. It is to reclaim the name of YHVH—the concept of God and the nature of reality—as a force for justice and stewardship of the earth. It is to proclaim at every opportunity that the world we have been given is a blessing and that the journey of liberation is built into the fabric of existence. We recognize our earth as a Garden of Eden, complete with abundant fruit trees and clear rivers running through it—enough food and water for everyone. It is up to us to lovingly protect and nurture this abundance in the name of YHVH. We recognize a world of spectacular human diversity—of genders and skin colors and shapes and physical abilities and gifts. We are blessed with people who make music and art; people who build things; people who explore the universe through science; people who explore the universe through meditation; people who grow vegetables; and people who work in factories. It is up to us to celebrate and promote this diversity in the name of YHVH.

We recognize a world of a stunning array of wildlife—at least 8.7 million species, with the majority not even yet identified, all inherently good. From elephants to earthworms to pelicans to plankton to gut flora to trees that breathe on behalf of all the earth, each has a unique role in the multilayered web of ecosystems that sustain life. It is up to us to find the humility to make space for this profusion of life in the name of YHVH.

We recognize that from among all the animals, we humans have been given the gift of intellect. We have the mental capacity to solve all the problems we've created— renewable energy systems to replace fossil fuel production, the social systems of safety nets to help those most in need, sustainable and humane agriculture, the understanding of supply chains and fair-trade practices that can offer workers a living wage. We even have the capacity to address many of the problems we haven't created— medicine to cure diseases, architecture to protect people from earthquakes. It's up to us to employ all of these capacities to heal the world in the name of YHVH.

Reclaiming Our Innocence

To keep the spirit of the third commandment, we need to extend ourselves beyond just the negative practice of not misusing the name of God or misrepresenting reality. The third commandment blesses the positive practice of claiming a vision of a loving, accepting, and forgiving God and a world that was inherently good from its inception and remains so.

Keeping the third commandment means we encounter violence and injustice in our lives and the world around us and reply that that's not the way the world is but the way we're making it through our actions. It is keeping the third commandment to assert when someone shoots up a school, that it's a *distortion*, not the *expression* of human nature. Humans from infancy show preference for fairness and kindness. Humans in every culture show compassion and empathy for others. To keep the third commandment is to say that our destruction of the environment is not due to our inherent selfishness but our shortsightedness, which can be corrected. When we stop pinning injustice and oppression on "reality" and instead take responsibility for it ourselves, we are keeping the third commandment. We humans may be behind the curve right now, but, in the words of Theodore Parker, "the arc of the moral universe bends toward justice."

A progressive movement grounded in a theology of wholeness and love—a positive vision of a world of blessing—would have great moral and political power. We would live in a world where God could be God and life could be life and the sanctity of these ideas—the inherent goodness and beauty of the universe—could shine among us. We would hold open the doors of possibility, taking every opportunity to proclaim that things can be different from the way they happen to be right now. By keeping the third commandment to protect the holiness of reality, we would spread joy, not mistrust; safety, not peril. We would care for one another in this way—giving hope where hope is often hard to find.

The sweetest fruit of this work of proclaiming the innocence of God in a suffering world is that we reclaim our own innocence as well. No one can ever convince us again that we are naïve or delusional or childish for believing that we can live together in love or nurture humans and the earth together. We will know that we have the power of YHVH within us and that ultimately the force of life and the essential promise of goodness are unimpeachable.

SHABBAT

▼

The Fourth Commandment

Observe the Sabbath Day
and Keep It Holy

▲

*Squander One Day
Every Week*

Observe the Sabbath day, to keep it holy, as YHVH your God commanded you. Six days you will labor and do all your work, but the seventh day is a Sabbath for YHVH your God. Do not do any work—you, or your son, or your daughter, or your male servant, or your female servant, or your ox, or your donkey, or any of your animals, or the stranger who is within your gates; so that your male servant and your female servant can rest like you.

"Terrifying." This was the word a congregant, David, used to describe his alarm when he was talking with a Jewish family and learned that they keep Shabbat (Sabbath) for a full day each week. They had explained that from sundown Friday until three stars are visible in the sky on Saturday evening, they don't work or spend money or run errands. They don't tackle problems or talk about thorny issues. They just relax, play with the kids, amble around the neighborhood, read, prepare nice meals and eat them together, invite friends over, and try to enjoy the abundance of all they already have. "That sounds terrifying," he said.

David is a law professor and he was undoubtedly reflecting on all the things he had to get done. Even this conversation was taking too long. It's hard enough, he must have been thinking, to get everything done in seven days. Subtracting a day a week would be catastrophic. The exams to grade, the next class to prepare, the dry cleaning to be dropped off, the research required to buy a new mattress, the taxes to be filed, the desperately needed haircut to procure, the hallway light bulb to be changed—all these feel immutable to him, as such things do to many of us. Sure, kick back for a couple hours on the weekend, watch a movie, go out for a meal—but a whole day? The same day? Every week? Impossible.

David is not alone in this reaction. Although Sabbath practice is one of the most plainly articulated commandments, very few of the "People of the Book" actually keep a Sabbath. Only traditionally observant Jews, Mormons, Seventh-Day Adventists, and a few other small Christian denominations even try. Maybe keeping this particular commandment is just too hard. And it's fascinating to think that it *is* so hard, because on the surface, it seems to be precisely the opposite. It seems designed to give us a break from hard things.

It's a commandment suggesting leisure, vacation, and enjoyment. Aren't these things, by definition, *easy*? Why would anyone need to be "commanded" to indulge in leisure?

Once We Were Slaves

To answer this question, we look back at the origin of Sabbath practice. It's no coincidence that the Sabbath was given to a people who, in their own self-understanding, had once been slaves. As the biblical story tells it, it was after the Israelites were enslaved in Egypt and escaped through the miraculous parting of the sea, after their liberation, on the clean slate of the desert landscape that the concept of Shabbat was born. God rained bread (*manna*) down to feed the people and instructed them through Moses to collect it only six days a week. On the sixth day they would find a double portion to collect, and on the seventh day they were to rest. This was a prototypical Sabbath, even before the revelation of the full Sabbath commandment on Mount Sinai.

The newly freed Israelites had the unique opportunity to establish a civilization from scratch—a pure social experiment. How should they organize their new world? What would it take to create a society free from the kinds of oppression, violence, cruelty, and excess that characterized the world they had left? What could ensure their freedom? The Ten Commandments were YHVH's answer to these questions, and the fourth commandment especially. To keep Shabbat was to declare defiance against the powers that had enslaved them or any that might try to enslave them in the future: one day a week, nothing and no one was going to make them work.

This was not as easy as it looked. Freedom from forced physical labor was just the first step. Shabbat meant claiming internal freedom as a second step, refusing to be a slave in one's own heart and mind. The Exodus text describes how the Israelites struggled to leave the trauma of slavery behind them and reimagine themselves as free people. They hoarded the *manna*, not trusting that it would be there the next day; they went out looking for it on Shabbat. They knew they needed to form a new identity—a sense of self beyond their identity as slaves. But it was hard to do and they resisted it. Their culture had been shaped by the life that had been imposed on them—the work they were forced to do as the price of their survival, the persecution they suffered, as well as the small perks they enjoyed: meat to eat and perhaps the predictability of their routines. Who were they now that they were no longer slaves?

What would they do with their time? Who would take care of them?

On more than one occasion, feeling scared and disoriented, they wailed to Moses that they would have been better off back in Egypt (Exodus 16:3). Once they began to actually hatch a plan to "appoint a chief and go back to Egypt" (Numbers 14:4). At times they expressed shared nostalgia for the days of slavery, saying, "We remember the fish that we used to eat in Egypt for free, the cucumbers and the melons and the leeks and the onions and the garlics" (Numbers 11:5).

Slavery Today

An estimated 21 million people today are victims of some kind of forced labor in the form of trafficked workers around the world. These people don't have the option of keeping this commandment and rehearsing their liberation. They are still trapped in the hell that the mythical Israelites in Egypt knew so well, unable to claim even a single day for themselves, denied the dignity of control over their own time. This is the existential horror of slavery, that a person's lifespan—the most precious thing we have on this earth—is stolen.

Those who are forced by financial necessity to work constantly suffer another form of slavery. The federal minimum wage is far below what a living wage would be in most states, meaning that working a full-time job is not even close to enough to keep a person out of poverty. The proverbial single mother who has to work night shifts and day shifts at multiple jobs struggling to keep food on the table for her kids often cannot afford a day or an afternoon of Sabbath rest. Today's trafficked workers and wage slaves cannot even attain step one of liberation—the crossing of the sea to physical freedom. Step two is barely conceivable.

You would think that those of us who *are* fortunate enough to live free and have the economic means to take a day off would relish the opportunity. You'd think we would be eager to take that second step toward internal, spiritual liberation. But generally we can't or won't. We may have the hypothetical freedom to do so, but we feel that we don't have the "time." This is doubly so if we follow the lead of the medieval rabbis and include in the concept of "work," not just work for pay, but any participation in the cycle of consumerism—buying, selling, striving, managing money, maintaining possessions, running errands...basically dealing with our stuff and getting stuff done.

We find it extraordinarily difficult to take a hiatus from all of this even one day out of seven. Apparently things haven't changed much in the last few thousand years. While the cessation of work might look easy on the surface, for the ancient Israelites as well as for modern, middle-class people in affluent nations, the shift in consciousness it requires is profound. This paradoxical difficulty of Sabbath practice is precisely what makes it so radical.

Divesting Oneself of Capitalism

At a workshop on Sabbath practice, a participant articulated this paradox perfectly. After a guided meditation that took people through a hypothetical Sabbath day, the group was asked to call out some of the benefits of having such a day each week. People rattled off a long list, including "relaxation," "time with family," "time alone," and so forth. Then one guy, a jovial character with a British accent and a wry smile, volunteered, "Divesting oneself of capitalism!" Apparently he experiences capitalism as a burden to be merrily cast off. But when the group was asked to generate a list of everything that would be *hard* about keeping a Sabbath day, the same guy called out again, "Divesting oneself of capitalism!" He nailed it on both counts.

Capitalism—or more specifically, corporate capitalism and the relentless consumerism and striving that accompany it—is the rapturous and lethal addiction of our time. We love it and we hate it. We love the intoxicating flow of pleasures that it brings us—Netflix, new clothes, ice cream in the summer and bananas in the winter, to name just a few. We love being able to improve and beautify ourselves—to have a "lifestyle" curated from a long list of ready-made choices. On the other hand, we have a vague sense that these privileges come at a cost. We find ourselves embroiled in an unending cycle of wanting more, getting more (or not), consuming more (if we can), and then wanting still more. We work long hours, commute long distances, and sleep way too little. Even weekends, for those lucky enough to have them, are typically spent in a frenzy of acquisition, preparation, consumption, and productivity. Stopping doesn't feel like an option. We have many things but no time.

We are also becoming increasingly aware of the costs of consumerism to our planet. The same economies that demand nonstop consumption from us humans demand nonstop production from the earth. Every one of the products and services we enjoy had its birthplace in some natural ingredient that, at some point in its history, was extracted from the land or oceans. The extraction never, ever stops. The law of Shabbat stipulates that all work cease on the seventh day, including that of farmers and animals, effectively giving the land time to regenerate. Later in the biblical text, the concept of the Sabbatical year is introduced: on the seventh year in every "week of years," humans are to let the land lie fallow, neither planting nor harvesting, and enter a kind of modified hibernation. Whether the Sabbatical year was ever fully observed is hard to know. But certainly today the idea would seem absurd. Corporations can't afford to lose a year's worth of profits; we can't afford to lose the time.

The Despotic Bell

Karl Marx, the nineteenth-century economist, had a great deal to say about time. At least one insight of his is incontrovertible: time is the ultimate form of human wealth. It is the measure of all things. To Marx, it's the labor time congealed in a product that gives it its "exchange value," or price. Regardless of whether this is literally accurate in economic terms, it is certain that our hours on this planet are all we've got and all we've got to give. We have one finite life on this planet now. We each live in the shadow of a ticking clock. None of us know when our time will be up. In Marx's writings, he describes how this precious human time no longer belongs to us as individuals; our time is broken down, appropriated, and devoured by the "boundless thirst" of capitalism. He describes the "despotic bell" of the workplace that wrenches people—mere "personifications of labor time"—from their homes. In capitalism, free time is a waste or, at best, just preparation for more productivity.

Marx's workers were destitute factory laborers—what today we might call sweatshop laborers—but his principle holds for workers in all tiers of our modern economy. He describes how technology, rather than freeing us from labor, creates an increasingly frenetic pace of work—the need to milk more and more value from a human hour, to "close the pores" of time. Certainly we recognize this today: that somehow in our high-tech world we are all still dizzyingly busy. Even when—or *especially* when—the "despotic bell" is the gentle chime of an iPhone, the workday never really ends. Because exactly as Marx described, any extra time created by labor-saving technology is immediately sucked back into the system to create more value—more money, more goods, more innovation. We never actually receive the extra time *as* time. We have to work harder and longer to make what we consider to be "a living."

It isn't as if we're unaware of this conundrum; we are aware and we worry about it. Time and its use are constant topics of conversation. The discussions circulate and recirculate of harried parents, always juggling, always feeling like they're letting someone down, not spending enough time with their kids and not spending enough time at the office. We struggle to get traction in various careers with less and less time to learn the craft. We hire experts in "time management" to help us gain control. We are so anxious about time slipping through our fingers.

Strangely, despite our anxiety (or because of it), in the free time we do allow ourselves, we often replace our real busyness with faux or vicarious busyness. We play fast-paced computer games or watch sports or reality TV shows. We shop for things we don't need, revise our workout regimen, watch a YouTube video of someone's cat sliding off a counter and then forward it to all our virtual friends. We get our nails done or our hair trimmed. We post our breakfast masterpiece to Facebook, retweet a joke about a politician's latest gaffe, and check our phones hundreds of times a day.

If we're honest with ourselves, these are not joyful, life-affirming, relationship-building, or spiritually deepening deployments of our time. They are seductive distractions that run down the clock. And it's strange that we're willing to run down the clock when we're so concerned about our mortality. Strange that we're so eager to kill time when we always feel like we have so little of it. Especially because, of course, we can't actually kill time: time kills us. Time continues inexorably regardless of what we do, and the universe seems indifferent to how we spend our lives. It's *we* who die and become, in Marx's words, "at best, time's carcass." We live in collective denial about this. Maybe the prospect of time running out is so terrifying that rather than try to reclaim our time for ourselves, we panic, turn, and run.

Sabbath Rules

Even those of us who concede all of this—who do wish we had more time for ourselves and families and who like the idea of Sabbath time—tend to be skeptical that a bunch of rules is necessary. A congregant, Joy, tells a story of what happened when she and her husband Joe decided that the Sabbath rules they had followed their whole lives were unnecessarily strict. As she tells it, the beginning of the end of her Sabbath practice came one Sunday when she realized they were out of cinnamon. Her Mormon faith taught that you don't go shopping on Sundays, but she needed cinnamon for the special meal she was preparing for her family. It was a key ingredient. So she discussed it with her husband and they decided that they would go just this once and just buy the cinnamon and nothing else. They would still stay internally in the spirit of the Sabbath the whole time. So they went out and bought the cinnamon and nothing terrible happened, no one got struck by lightning, and they had their meal.

Joy has happy memories of Sabbath with her family growing up. They went to church in the morning, baked cookies in the afternoon, listened to special music, made dinner all together and then spent hours at the table, just hanging out talking and being silly and laughing. Sunday nights they would all pile onto their parents' bed and watch G-rated movies. When she left home, Joy missed those family Sundays. But as she grew older, she moved away from Mormonism— among other things, she objected to LDS's conservative stances on gay marriage and gender roles. The Sabbath rules, along with all religious rules, had come to feel less important—hence, the cinnamon incident.

The next week it was cheese. "It would be so nice to have some cheese to go with dinner tonight; let's go out and just get some cheese. Nothing else." While they were at the store, they picked up some bread too. To go with the cheese. Again, no lightning. The next Sunday, it was, "Well, while we're here at the store we might as well just zip around and do a little shopping for the week, just a quick one to get us through since we're out of a bunch of stuff." You can imagine how it progressed, Sunday after Sunday. Food shopping became a regular fixture of the day, then laundry. They told each other, "We're still keeping the spirit of the Sabbath with our special meal and special Sabbath music."

Joe was fighting a deadline one Sunday and needed to do just a little work. Joy decided, "If he's working... I might as well get something done too." Now they were both working and shopping and running errands on Sundays. Their special dinners fell away and the special music fell away. And pretty soon Sunday became, in Joy's words, "just another day." And it was right around that time when they noticed that they were experiencing their lifetime peak of Sunday-night anxiety. They used to coast to the end of their Sabbath feeling rested and centered. Now they were getting things done on Sundays, but they had never felt more stressed. By Sunday night they were tired, fighting with each other, overwhelmed. For the first time in their lives, they felt like they could hardly face the week ahead.

Joy and Joe's cautionary tale makes a strong case for "rules." They assumed that a small purchase on the Sabbath would be harmless, when in fact it wound up chipping away at their spiritual practice until there was nothing left. It is said that absolute abstinence is easier than perfect moderation. Making exceptions and partial commitments to a practice can actually be much harder than staying in with both feet. Had Joy and Joe been able to continue to observe these seemingly arbitrary rules, they might have preserved something that was precious to them both.

A Person Will Worship Something

Joy and Joe's story exposes the commonly held falsehood that once we reject religious laws, we are no longer bound by any laws at all. Actually we often become bound by the laws of capitalism and secular culture, inadvertently and by default. Ralph Waldo Emerson's quote from the introduction bears repeating here: "A person will worship something—have no doubt about that. We may think our tribute is paid in secret in the dark recesses of our hearts—but it will out. That which dominates our imaginations and our thoughts will determine our lives, and character. Therefore, it behooves us to be careful what we worship, for what we are worshipping, we are becoming." Like it or not, we will worship something. We will be bound by something. And just as secular culture offers freedom from religion's laws, religious law offers freedom from secular culture's laws.

The fourth commandment calls for a Sabbath "to"

or "for" YHVH. When the Israelites leave Egypt in the biblical story, they don't become "free" in the sense of being able to do whatever they want. The Pharaoh merely gets replaced by God as their ruler. New restrictions replace the old. It sounds like a case of "meet the new boss, same as the old boss." But the key difference is that this God—this ruler—is YHVH. It is being itself. The fourth commandment enjoins us to keep a Sabbath for being itself—our own inner being, cosmic being, the state of being. We reserve one day out of seven to simply be.

This sense of the Sabbath as an airy, mystical time to simply be is most beautifully described by the twentieth-century Polish-American rabbi Abraham Joshua Heschel. He shared Marx's insight that time is the ultimate form of human wealth. In his 1951 book *The Sabbath*, Heschel writes about Shabbat—the mirror image of Marx's dystopia—a time devoted to prayer, family, community, pleasure, and awe. His famous metaphor for Shabbat was "a palace in time." Like a physical palace in space, you can only enter it by leaving the rest of the world behind. And once you are inside, it is spectacular, spacious, and bejeweled in a way that you could never imagine from the outside. On this one day of the week, the "pores of time" open and the world breathes. Heschel writes in the language of bliss and surrender.

And while Heschel didn't necessarily intend to write a political text, he clearly suggests that there's a contest for loyalty here. The sociopolitical battleground is staked out. Heschel writes,

> He who wants to enter the holiness of the day must first lay down the profanity of clattering commerce, of being yoked to toil. He must go away from the screech of dissonant days, from the nervousness and fury of acquisitiveness and the betrayal in embezzling his own life.

Embezzling One's Own Life

What does it mean to embezzle one's life? Per Wikipedia, embezzlement is "the act of withholding assets for the purpose of theft by an individual to whom such assets have been entrusted, to be used for other purposes." The asset in question here is time. Heschel is warning that when we stay embroiled in commerce day in and day out, we are stealing *time*, which has been entrusted to us by YHVH to be used for other purposes. This concept brings us back to the metaphor of YHVH as ruler. Time belongs to Being itself. Some portion of it must remain sacred and cannot be sold for any earthly sum.

The commandment is clear that we cannot cheat and recruit any surrogates for productivity—our children, our employees, animals, or even foreign visitors. Sabbath is for everyone. This is why Sabbath observance is a spiritual practice: it takes discipline, ironically, to enter into an undisciplined, formless time. It takes courage to assert and reassert our freedom. And it takes compassion to extend that freedom to others in our lives.

As sweet and gentle as the Sabbath may be, its arrival collides violently with the secular world. It forces us to choose every week: Will I embezzle time from YHVH or will I surrender to a deeper principle of joy and meaning? It forces us to confront the question, *To whom or to what do I ultimately belong?* As we become more and more able to answer, "I belong to YHVH" or "to my deepest self" or "to the world community" or "to the earth," we grow in spiritual strength. The tension between the call of work and the call of the Sabbath becomes weight added to our spiritual barbells—another opportunity to destabilize our ordinary world and lift up our deepest truths.

In secular culture we may belong to our work or to money or to our quest to lose ten pounds or to our need to gain status or be "liked." Our social and political systems hinge on our belief that these priorities are natural and immutable. Free time has to squeeze in around these priorities. When the Sabbath comes along and insists that in fact *it* is immutable and all else is negotiable, the world is turned inside out. It is this non-negotiability that gives the fourth commandment its countercultural power. Traditionally, exceptions are made only for emergencies threatening life or health. Everything else—everything else!—comes to a screeching halt at sundown. A check might be left half-written, a shopping trip abandoned with an empty cart, the writing of a paper stopped midsentence. This is where the personal gets political. Sabbath practice injects doubt into dominant logic of capitalist culture. For "a thought," in Heschel's words, "has blown the marketplace away."

Enoughness

Authors Joseph Heller and Kurt Vonnegut were talking together at the lavish party of a rich hedge fund manager. Kurt Vonnegut quipped, "You know, this guy who owns this mansion probably made more money this week than you've ever made from your decades of sales of *Catch-22*."

Joseph Heller replied, "Ah, but I have something that he will never have."

"What's that?" asked Vonnegut.

"Enough," said Heller.

The feeling of "enoughness" is the dividend of Sabbath practice. In Heschel's language, once we are no longer engaged in the "fury of acquisitiveness," then we can truly "enter the holiness of the day." We access a whole different dimension of life. By renouncing work and shopping for a day, we find that, as long as we have food, clean water, shelter, and health care, we have enough. And by renouncing striving and self-improvement for a day, we find that we *are* enough. We are free to spend our time for the sacred purposes for which it was given: awe, joy, connection, and love. We rediscover pure play, unmediated by our social institutions. We nurture the spiritual hippie child within. Jewish tradition teaches that we even get a "new soul" for the day. It's a new kind of consciousness.

Jewish families may light candles, linger over meals, play music, visit with friends, talk, pray, and nap. Others of us may go wandering—walk out our front door and take turns deciding whether to go right, left, or straight. We chat with people we encounter. There is no destination and no rush. Shayna, an observant Jew, when she goes out walking on Shabbat afternoon, carries no wallet or cell phone. She needs neither at that moment: she has enough. She describes loving the slightly naked feeling of being without these social anchors and the practice of trust in the people around her. There are almost limitless possibilities in the time palace—so many delicious ways to be unproductive. In Jewish tradition, Shabbat is considered a particularly wonderful and auspicious time to have sex with one's spouse. Some religious communities, like Seventh-Day Adventists and Mormons, stay at church all day, praying, eating, singing, eating some more, and just being together in community.

Sabbath: A Threat to Our Way of Life

You might notice from these examples that there is an element of charade involved in Sabbath practice. We can only eat Sabbath meals without shopping because we shopped beforehand. We can only go out without our cell phone because we have made arrangements to do so in advance. Sabbath is not a sustainable way to live, nor would most of us want it to be. It's analogous to city dwellers who go camping, setting up their tents and sleeping bags and s'more-making materials in advance so they can have a comfortable time in the wilderness. But Sabbath should never be mistaken for just an ordinary vacation either. The goal of a Sabbath practice is not to give us a joy ride and then patch us up and send us back out to the rat race. It is to represent in the *now* what freedom feels like, what connection with others feels like, what reverence for the earth feels like, and what *enough* feels like.

By lifting up a holy vision of the world and giving this brief but regular experience of redemption, the Sabbath can perform deeply political work: it can build an "outside" to society. Suddenly we have a vantage point from which to witness our lives. Without a practice like this, the secular, capitalist world is the only world there is. Its values, its goals, its appraisal of our successes and failures fill the horizon in every direction. There is literally nowhere *else*.

But now, with the Sabbath, each week there is somewhere else to go. Each week, we experience the pleasure of surrender to something larger than ourselves. Each week we feel the joy of contentment with what we already have—a quality of joy that, if it spread, would end our ruthless consumption of resources and heal our relationship with the earth. Our own social and economic structures become newly visible because we now have something to compare them to. Injustices now feel more unjust; cloying simulations of caring seem more disingenuous; abuse of our ecosystems and cruelty to living creatures become nauseating. The self that emerges from a full Sabbath and reenters the week is a changed self.

Does this radical transformation always or even

usually happen in Sabbath-keeping communities today? No. But the idea with its revolutionary potential has been passed down to us through the generations from the mythical time of the Israelites in the desert. We receive Shabbat like an unexploded grenade. It's a grenade of joy and love and freedom, but it's a grenade nonetheless. It's crackling with the potential energy to wreak havoc on everything. People understand this intuitively. That's what makes it scary. When we create breathing space in our week, all kinds of unwelcome feelings and thoughts can arise—feelings that we would rather leave buried under a mountain of tasks and momentary pleasures. We fear what would happen if these feelings became unbearable. For anyone interested in maintaining the social and political status quo or in sticking with their familiar routines, "terror," as David the law professor put it, is indeed the appropriate reaction. Sabbath is, in the best possible way, a threat to our way of life.

It's a paradox, but as with so many of the commandments, the fourth commandment is about freedom. The Sabbath was conceived by a people with ancestral memories of having once been slaves. The genius of their insight was that sometimes the most spiritually and politically radical use of time is not to spend it efficiently, but to squander it—to spend it lavishly, to while it away, as if the present moment were an eternity, as if the present moment were all there is, as if we had all the time in the world. This insight became enshrined in the Torah and henceforth the Israelites made perennial commitments to a liberating power even greater than the Pharaoh. Imagine if we made commitments to a liberating power greater than the Pharaohs of our day. Imagine if we reaffirmed those commitments every week with a community dedicated to reclaiming the wealth of time and the promise of justice for ourselves and for all the creatures of the earth. Imagine what it would be like to taste true freedom.

IMMA

▼

The Fifth Commandment

Honor Your Father and Your Mother

▲

Stay Accountable to Where You Came From

Honor your father and your mother so that your days will be long on the land that YHVH, your God, is giving you.

To make a baby, according to the ancient Near Eastern understanding of the reproductive process, you need three ingredients: the mother's seed, the father's seed, and God. The mother and father each make their contribution in the customary way and then God conjures the gestation by congealing the two human elements, like the effect of rennet to make cheese. Specifically, the father was thought to contribute the bones, the veins, the nails, the brain, and the white of the eye. The mother was thought to contribute the skin, muscles, blood, hair, and the pupil of the eye. God supplied the breath, soul, light in our faces, sight, hearing, speech, touch, sense, insight, and understanding.

A more modern understanding might be that the biological parents provide the physical elements—the DNA and proteins that create embryo, then fetus, then baby—and God provides the spirit or consciousness.

Parents make the hardware; God makes the software. Either way, the parents are seen as cocreators with God. This is the context of the biblical commandment to "honor your father and mother." This commandment appears in the *first* half of the commandments, the half that generally has to do with our relationship with God, rather than where one might expect it to be, in the second half, which pertains to our relationships with humans. In Jewish tradition the honoring of parents and the honoring of God are closely intertwined. They are spiritual practices of honoring our Source in all its many forms.

This all sounds a little heteronormative for our understanding of family these days. We know today that biology and parenthood are often two different things. Children are raised by same-sex couples, single parents, adoptive parents, relatives, or friends. And this was also true in biblical days, where orphaned children, so-called illegitimate children, and many other categories of children were raised by people other than biological parents. This commandment would have been equally binding to them. Honor the people who parented us, regardless of whether or not they are the same people who contributed our genetic material to the magical soup in the womb. The act of creation of a person doesn't end at birth. In many ways it has just begun.

The essence of parenting is what happens once you have a real-life breathing, arguing, squirming person in your arms.

It's Complicated

For many of us, the idea of honoring our parents is not a straightforward proposition. It's complicated. It conjures mixed feelings, old resentments, love, and guilt. And being *commanded* to honor them is even more uncomfortable. Some might say in response, "You obviously don't know my mother." And indeed our parents may have been abusive or neglectful or emotionally unavailable. Our parents might have not really seen us, not had time for us. We may not trust or like them. We may never have known them or never have been claimed by a parent. One or both parents might have abandoned us entirely. Or they may not be alive anymore, which makes the whole topic even more fraught. For some of us, the rejection of our parents has been a crucial step in claiming our own selfhood—an act of empowerment that still has deep meaning years later.

The commandment to honor one's father and mother seems to threaten a precious space we worked hard to carve out for ourselves. Because of all this, the Talmud (a collection of rabbinic writings that interpret and expand the Torah's laws) calls this commandment the most difficult one in the Torah.

The fifth commandment does not require us to deny the ways our parents hurt us. Nor does it ask us to exonerate them from their failed responsibility. It does not require us to pretend to have feelings that we don't have or compromise our hard-won boundaries. It does not ask us to forgive what we find unforgivable. It does not even require us to stay in relationship with a parent when, as in some cases of abuse, a clean break is necessary for our healing.

The commandment does seem to require one to care materially for one's parents should they need it, according to one midrash, "even to go begging at men's doors, if he cannot otherwise maintain his parents."

Interpreted more broadly, the fifth commandment calls us to cultivate the very un-American quality of humility. It asks us to acknowledge that we are not self-made. We are products of all that came before us, including the flawed love of our parents, the successes and failures of our ancestors, the teachers of all kinds who have shaped us throughout our lives. Our parents are a vital piece of who we are today, in both good and bad ways. Some of us may have followed closely in their footsteps. Others of us may be living a negative response to our upbringing—influenced in exactly opposite ways from how our parents intended. Most of us are somewhere in between—striving to chart our own course through life. We are indebted to our parents for much of what we think of as our "selves." And so the fifth commandment teaches that we owe them respect, material care, and as much gratitude as we can muster.

Along with the challenges all parents bequeathed us, they gave us gifts. To honor our parents is to honor the good in ourselves that was nurtured by those gifts. Whatever our parents' failings, most of them loved us exactly as well as they were able. Like all of us, they were limited (and supported) by their own parents and past experiences. And despite their limitations, they—or someone—cared for each of us when we were babies. They fed us, clothed us, held us, kept us clean—at least somewhat—or we would not be alive today. Human infants are the most fragile of all animal babies—a newborn cannot survive even a day without food and care. At the very least, we received this much from our parents or their surrogate caregivers.

The Hebrew word *imma* means "mother." In many languages, the word is similar—*amma, mama, maman, ema, mamai*—simple, elemental sounds that a baby can make. In any language, it represents less a person than an idea: the primal relationship and source of nurturing for all of us. It signifies the love on which we utterly depend.

Imma is embodied in human beings—women and men—who give such love to another. To honor our parents is to honor that love and ground ourselves in the reality of our contingency in this world. We are indebted to them for our lives. We would not be here if not for our parents.

Don't Dis Your Past

Once we embrace this stark truth, the regrets we may have about how they parented us or how we "turned out" begin to take on a different hue. In an interview with Rabbi Zalman Schachter-Shalomi when he was eighty-nine years old, he talks extensively about what it means to be in the December of life, looking back on one's many decades here on earth and contemplating death. He is asked, "How do you work with regret?" He seems to get very excited about the question. This is clearly something to which he has given a lot of thought. In his answer, he refers to regret as a kind of disrespect to one's past. He assumes the voice of the past self talking to the current self, saying, "Don't dis me. The person you are now wouldn't exist if it hadn't been for the person I was then." In another sense, then, too, we are contingent in this world. We are indebted to our past for our existence and for our existence as the people we are.

It's so easy to look back on our lives and wish that

things could have been different. If only we had done x, y, and z instead of a, b, and c, life would be great. If only our parents had done this or that differently, we'd be so much better off...so much happier, so much richer, so much smarter. We'd have a partner. We wouldn't be anxious. We wouldn't have this addiction or that eating disorder. But Schachter-Shalomi teaches that this line of thinking is debilitating. And it's unintelligible. We can't know how our lives would have gone if some factor had been different in our past. We can only know ourselves today as the living product of a marbled history, all the ways in which we were loved and the ways in which we were abandoned, all our successes and missteps, all our hard work and all our bad luck, all our pain and all our good luck.

To say that our parents are only worthy of honoring to the extent that they were "good parents" is to say that we are only worth honoring to the extent that *we* are good. Honoring our mother and father is a way of honoring the entirety of the life that has made us who we are. It's a way of honoring ourselves.

Maybe to make a baby you need just three ingredients, but to make an adult you need millions. Countless people, countless moments have collaborated in our formation. We have been parented by the world. Nurtured, disciplined and at times failed by life itself, here we are, the deeply flawed and beautiful children of that process. We could reinterpret the fifth commandment to say, instead of just "Honor your mother and father," "Honor all of that which has made you *you*." To be able to honor that which is imperfect—our parents, our histories, and our world—is to honor the truth of who we are. In the end, it is to offer ourselves an unconditional embrace.

"Can I Donate My Kidney against My Parent's Wishes?"

In the "Ask the Rabbi" column of a Chabad website, an observant Jew poses the question of whether it is permissible to donate his kidney even though his mother does not want him to. The situation is a conundrum because it sets two *mitzvot* (commandments) into conflict with each other: the commandment to honor father and mother versus the commandment to save a life. The rabbi begins by addressing the question of whether we are obligated to risk our own life to save another's life and, while there is disagreement in the texts about this, concludes that in this case the man is not obligated by Jewish law to donate his kidney. On the other hand, kidney donation is quite safe these days. The risk is low and the man *wants* to do it. So then the question becomes, is it a violation of the fifth commandment for him to do something—*anything*—that his mother does not want him to do?

The rabbi concludes that it is not. He writes, "While you are obligated to honor your parents and fulfill their wishes, you are not obligated to do so if what they are asking is not something that will necessarily affect or benefit them." In other words, if the man's mother had kidney disease and needed a kidney, and he was opting to give his kidney to someone else instead of to her, that would be a violation of the commandment. But her mere discomfort with the idea of him doing it is not enough to require him to fulfill her wishes.

This interpretation brings beautiful nuance to this commandment. To honor one's parents does not mean to obey them. We are only obligated to fulfill our parents' wishes in matters that materially affect them. This leaves to our own discretion the entire galaxy of decisions pertaining to our own lives and how we operate in the political and social world. Parents may disagree that their children's lives don't affect them. Many parents' identities are so deeply entwined with those of their children that anything the child does, even as an adult, can be experienced as something that affects the parents. But the rabbi in this case puts that determination in the hands of the adult child.

This places each one of us in charge of navigating

all the tensions that inevitably arise between keeping the fifth commandment and keeping the others. Such tensions will come up frequently because, as we've seen with the first four commandments, keeping the commandments and living a spiritually grounded life often necessitates violating social norms. Parents are often keepers of these norms. To keep the first commandment and have no other gods before YHVH, we may have to demote our parents' gods, whether they be the Denver Broncos, the Metropolitan Opera, or the United States of America. To keep the second commandment and not make and worship idols, we may have to shed our parents' values—the image of material success, the performance of class or gender, or the inflated display of one's achievements. To keep the third commandment and not take the name of YHVH in vain, we may have to reject our parents' warnings about "the real world" and seek to reclaim our innocence. And to keep the fourth commandment and observe a Sabbath, we may have to relinquish beloved family traditions around consumption, work, and entertainment.

Differentiation Is a Prerequisite

Double-click on a parent and we find the social and political worlds that have shaped us—a heritage that is in some cases rich and beautiful and in others oppressive or even violent. Our parents represent so much more than just their individual presence as people in our lives. They are the conduits for culture. They are the first to teach us, by word and by example, what's "normal." Their parenting style and their own faith transmit a powerful theology to us—we learn whether the universe is loving or harsh, whether we are fundamentally okay or fundamentally inadequate, whether God exists or is a wishful figment of the imaginations of weak people. We learn from them first what gender means and what the color of our skin means. Some of us have spent a lifetime trying to disentangle ourselves from those worlds we inherited. Nowhere is the personal more political than in the work we do to question the assumptions we drank from the bottle and breast.

Imagine a gay man whose evangelical parents sent him to "conversion therapy" and who grew up attending a church in which the message pounding weekly from that pulpit was that gays were going to hell. If he is to thrive or even survive in this world, have loving, stable relationships, and grow up to fight for the rights of others, he must somehow disentangle from the deep sense of shame he felt sitting with his dad in those church pews.

If the environmental activist decides to become vegan, she must disentangle from the love she felt as her *imma* cooked chicken soup for the family and the warm, almost intoxicating smell filled the apartment. If the shy child from Alabama grows up and wants to become a gun control advocate, he must somehow disentangle from the sense of belonging and pride he felt when his grandfather handed him his first gun—a Remington 870 Wingmaster—at age fifteen and told him that now he was a man.

The commandment to honor father and mother allows us to honor the people we have become as adults and requires us to be able to separate ourselves from our parents. It challenges us to know where their wishes merely reflect their own cultural biases (which we may have inherited and then rejected) and to know where they have a legitimate claim on our attention and behavior. To keep the fifth commandment requires us to have a relationship with God/reality that exists independently of our relationship with our parents—to know right from wrong even when they do not and to see the world through a lens other than theirs. We must know where they end and where we begin. Differentiation is a prerequisite to keeping this commandment. After we have separated out what we do *not* owe our parents (i.e., pretending to be straight, eating chicken soup, or going to gun shows on weekends), this commandment calls us to lovingly and humbly give them what we do.

Leaving Where We Came From

The other option, of course, is just to leave. Some of us leave our families entirely. Our nation is comprised mostly of descendants of those who left something behind to find a better life. With the significant exception of enslaved Africans, who were kidnapped and forced, and native peoples, who were already here, our various ancestors made this journey voluntarily, immigrating from a faraway home to find religious freedom or financial security, or as refugees fleeing violence. Americans tend to leave where we came from and don't look back.

We have relocated culturally and intellectually as well, generally moving from more conservative to more liberal, from less freedom to more. That gay marriage went from impossible to inevitable in the United States in such a short time span is a testament to the strength of this current: household by household, gay people became human in the eyes of the American public. Their commitments to one another came to be seen as real commitments, their parenting as real parenting, their love as real love. Likewise, in one generation it was acceptable to fight openly for segregated schools and buses; in the next generation it wasn't. In one generation you could argue with a straight face that women should be ineligible to vote; in the next generation you couldn't.

Leaving where we came from and not looking back is also our practice of religion. It is becoming almost traditional to leave one's family's faith. Some find the scriptures and sermons irrelevant to modern life or, at worst, regressive. They point to violent biblical narratives or religious traditions in conservative Christianity and Orthodox Judaism and judge religion as unforgivable and irredeemable. They want no part of it.

When a primary relationship gets hard, when someone (like a parent) or something (like a religious tradition) does something inexcusable, and when our values seem incommensurate with theirs, leaving can be the easiest option. It may be painful, but it's clean and simple. To justify it to ourselves, we usually have to paint the person or tradition as unequivocally and irredeemably bad in our minds. We have to envision that this "badness" goes down to their core. We have to imagine that they are incapable of change or that any change they could possibly make would be far too little far too late. And we have to imagine we are not really *of* them; that once we break away, we will be free from whatever negative qualities and influence they embody. We will attain that all-American feeling of empowerment, forging into the future and leaving behind whatever "isn't working for us." We will be able to proceed with our lives unencumbered.

Unfortunately, it doesn't often work out that way. It is impossible to build a wall where "we" are on one side and "they" are on the other. Every time we build a wall, something we love winds up on the other side. As empowering as it may feel to abandon anachronistic and painful traditions, there is also an incalculable loss. Like abandoning parents who were deeply flawed, to abandon our birth traditions is to abandon a part of ourselves. We cut ourselves and our children off from a heritage that has been passed down for generations, like cutting a limb off an ancient sequoia. For better or worse, religious and cultural traditions are woven deeply into our being. Their memes are braided into our emotional and sensory memories and even our most private experiences of God and life. By denying this, we fool ourselves. We also hamper our ability to recognize and understand how those memes travel and flow in us. We cannot really grapple with what we pretend isn't there. If we try to cut off every problematic branch of our being, we become a diminished, alien version of ourselves.

In the process we flatten out a complex, multilayered tradition and reduce it to one homogenous, unpleasant slab of matter. We say, "You're not that complicated to figure out. I've got your number. I can net out in thirty seconds what you have taken millennia to become." We indulge in the hubris of thinking that we know better than what has been learned from thousands of years of evolving tradition, sacred stories whose meanings have expanded and morphed, generations of interpretations and reinterpretations, activists who have rebelled and reformed the faith time and again, mystics who have spent their lives plumbing the depths of one particular spiritual well, scholars who have written volumes, and contemporary theologians working and reworking the raw material of faith. And as we take our ball and go home from the game of religion, we relinquish our place in that transgenerational conversation. The evolving tradition is now deprived of our insights and spirit and contemporary sensibilities.

Wrestle but Stay in the Game

To take our ball and go home is, in a sense, lazy. Rather than ask the hard questions about how and where to locate ourselves in the tradition and how and where to extricate ourselves, today's progressives tend to sweep everything about religion off the table. Then we put a few items back on based on nostalgia, aesthetics, and a secular notion of what's "reasonable." We might still erect a Christmas tree, for example, or produce a sanitized, short-form Passover Seder.

We think we are just keeping the good parts, but often we are keeping the parts that make fewest demands on us. Meanwhile we miss out on the actual good parts—the wisdom, the spiritual guidance, the challenge to transform our world, the discipline, and the archetypal stories that can help us make sense of our lives. We miss the tools for understanding and paths for spiritual growth. Perhaps most importantly we miss out on the prophetic dimension of religion—theological resources to counter the logic of the secular world. The Ten Commandments are one such resource and there are countless others.

None of this is to say that the violent and patriarchal dimensions of religious traditions should be excused or ignored. Nor should they be complied with or perpetuated. Remember, the fifth commandment does not require us to obey in all cases but to *honor* our parents. We can donate a kidney even if they don't want us to. Doing what our religious tradition "doesn't like" in the name of a higher purpose is kosher. We can and should rebel against every part of religion that is harmful or spiritually bankrupt—everything that we can identify as mere products of regressive human social norms. But rather than sweep everything off the table and then put a few elements back on, we honor our traditions by beginning with a full table and removing elements or changing them only if and when they prove to be oppressive.

As we are called to honor our parents with compassion for their profound flaws, we are challenged to honor the insights of the past and institutions that were our progenitors, with compassion for their failures. We pass them on to our children (albeit perhaps differently from how they were passed down to us)—with reverence and gratitude for the gifts they bring and with our eyes wide open to their deficits and dangers.

The word "Israel" comes from a Hebrew phrase that means "wrestles with God." This is what we are called to do—to wrestle but to stay in the game. To wrestle with a parent or tradition in a way that combines investment with resistance is to keep this fifth commandment with great dignity.

Honoring the Earth, Our Primal *Imma*

The fifth commandment is one of only two commandments that offer a reason for keeping them. In this case, the reason seems at first glance to have nothing to do with the content of the commandment. "Honor your father and your mother *so that your days will be long on the land that YHVH, your God, is giving you.*" What would honoring parents have to do with the length of one's days on the land? This language suggests yet another layer to this teaching.

Parent, particularly mother, has been a metaphor for earth since early human societies. The term "mother earth" or "mother nature" appeared as early as the twelfth or thirteenth century BCE in Mycenaean Greek writings, around the same time or earlier than the Ten Commandments were first committed to papyrus. It's a common metaphor from indigenous cultures throughout the ages to the modern-day Gaia hypothesis of the living earth. The Jewish concept of the Shechinah encompasses both the divine feminine and the immanent or physical manifestation of the divine in this world. There is a universal human intuition that the earth is our ultimate parent—the earth birthed us and nurtures us and provides us all we need.

With this understanding of "parent," the fifth commandment addresses our relationship to the earth itself. We are to cherish the oceans that birth life; the soil that grows all our food; the rain forests that serve as the breath of the planet; the unfathomable array of animals, plants, and insects that all work together in delicate balance; and the ecosystems and atmosphere that create the perfect conditions—the only possible conditions—for our survival. We are to recognize ourselves as merely a part of an interdependent web of life, although the natural world as a whole is not at all dependent on humans for its welfare. She would be better off without us. In the postindustrial world, humans are not a productive part of the food chain; we do not contribute anything to the ecosystems in which we live. The dependency only runs one way. Seen through this lens, the fifth commandment calls us to humility before nature.

The explanation "so that your days might be long on the land" now makes more sense. If we treat Mother Earth with the quality of care and respect due to our own human mother, treading gently, replanting, helping her to heal, and living within our ecological means, the earth will shower us with her abundance and we will be able to live and thrive for many years to come. Animal species that are languishing will surge back, our climate will restabilize, our air will become clean for breathing and our water clean for drinking, there will be no more toxins poisoning our earth and sickening our families, and our days will be long on this land.

If we don't—if we continue to recklessly take and take from the earth to feed our consumer addictions— we will soon see oceans without fish, continents without forests, poles without glaciers, and gardens without bees, birds, or flowers. Then our days on this land will be quite a bit shorter.

Depending on Half the World before Breakfast

We are utterly dependent on the earth's systems in all their irreducible complexity. We are utterly dependent on the people immediately around us and the millions we will never meet who provide the food we eat, the medicines we need, and the material things we rely on to live in the modern world. We're utterly dependent on parents for the physical materials that formed our bodies and the teachings that shaped our minds and hearts. We are constituted by things and forces that come from outside ourselves. Rev. Martin Luther King Jr. preached, "Before you've finished eating breakfast in the morning, you've depended on half the world."

In an economic rendering, Senator Elizabeth Warren said,

There is nobody in this country who got rich on his own—nobody. You built a factory out there? Good for you. But I want to be clear. You moved your goods to market on the roads the rest of us paid for. You hired workers the rest of us paid to educate. You were safe in your factory because of police-forces and fire-forces that the rest of us paid for. You didn't have to worry that marauding bands would come and seize everything at your factory... because of the work the rest of us did.

This concept of our dependency and indebtedness to others and to the earth—and the obligations that it generates—flies in the face of one of the most cherished of American myths: the myth of the "self-made man." In our culture, the most successful person is the person who does it supposedly without help. He pulls himself up by his bootstraps. Someone who becomes a CEO without having gone to college earns special admiration. A solo artist is hailed as a "genius" more than a collaborative team. We are meant to forge our own way through life. And businesses and corporations that succeed must maintain the illusion that they did it without leaning on anyone or anything. But as Elizabeth Warren's quote points out, nothing could be further from the truth. And her list only included public goods, like roads and police forces; it did not even begin to enumerate the natural assets of the earth (which "the rest of us" will also pay for), extracted for free by that same factory.

This is the ethic of corporate capitalism—we aggressively use up everything we have and then, if we think we can get a better deal elsewhere, we leave. We behave as sui generis individuals, with little loyalty to where we came from and little accountability to what (and whom) we used to arrive where we are. The spiritual principle invoked by the commandment to honor your father and mother gets political at exactly this juncture. It contests this arrogance. Whatever the particular object of our honoring, whether it's our parents, the people around us, the traditions of our heritage, or the earth itself, this commandment insists on an orientation of humility and gratitude toward the world around us. It insists that we owe our very selfhood to others. We are to treat everything we touch with reverence.

This reverence, this honoring, means that we fiercely protect the natural gifts of the earth; we stay in relationship with our families and work to make them more loving; we stay in community with our faith and cultural traditions and work to help them evolve. We support wholeheartedly the public institutions that make possible all of our work in the world. We cultivate awe in the magnificent complexity of our universe, humbly acknowledging all that we do not know. We look for teachers, flawed though they may be, and we honor them. To keep this commandment is to live our lives in loving accountability to all that gave us the gift of life and to actively care for all that sustains it.

LO TIRTZACH

▼

The Sixth Commandment

Do Not Kill

▲

Renounce Human and Ecological Violence

Do not kill.

Ah, the old "thou shalt not kill." So pleasantly noncontroversial. So easy to agree to; so easy to comply with; so accessible; so unambiguous; so comfortably devoid of any ancient, exotic religious weirdness. Right? The sixth commandment is especially vanilla if you translate the Hebrew verb *tirtzach*, as many do, as "murder" rather than "kill." Then we're only talking about the stuff of whodunit mystery novels. We're not talking about killing in self-defense. We're not talking about killing in war. We're not talking about eating a beef burger. We're only talking about unprovoked, premeditated murder of a human being. We could find easy consensus that such murder is a bad thing and that we should be commanded to not do it.

The vast majority of us never would anyway. While we may occasionally fantasize about it, we will never *actually* put a gun to a forehead and pull the trigger or slide a knife into a stomach. And we don't do these things, not because we're commanded not to, but because we're naturally, powerfully inclined not to. It would nauseate us. It would cause us untold cognitive dissonance. Even soldiers who kill for a just cause can suffer PTSD and what's known as "moral injury" from the horrific experience of having taken the life of another human being. For reasons biological, social, and spiritual, killing goes against every fiber of our being.

The Ten Commandments are practical: They address inclinations that we actually have and deeds that we actually do. They guide us where, with the right intention and inspiration and teaching, we might choose a better path. To understand *lo tirtzach* narrowly as "do not murder" would make it a virtually meaningless commandment. Those who could hear it wouldn't need it, because they are not naturally inclined to murder. Those who needed it would be unable to hear it. (For example, the man who killed nine people in the Charleston church massacre evidently *is* inclined to murder and whatever compelled him to commit such an atrocity, no commandment could have made a difference.) This commandment is more complicated than that.

Here is a sampling of how the medieval commentators engaged its complexity:

Rabbi Ibn Ezra: "Do not murder, either physically or by your speech by lying, gossiping, deliberately giving fatal advice; or failing to reveal a secret that might save a life. If you do not reveal it, you are like a murderer."

Rabbi Hizkuni: "Do not murder, even by remaining silent when a murderer's plans become known to you. In fact, it really means 'Do not kill,' whether justly or unjustly."

Rabbi Abarbanel: "The prohibitions of murder, adultery, and theft are undoubtedly not single commandments, but headings that contain many commandments under them."

Rabbi Nachmanides offers a poetic gloss, speaking in God's voice: "Do not vandalize my creation by spilling human blood."

These commentators all define *lo tirtzach* more broadly to include indirect killing, passive killing, and simply letting someone die when you could save them. A passage of Leviticus that roughly paraphrases the Ten Commandments supports this interpretation with the warning, "Do not stand idly by the blood of your neighbor." This is often understood to mean that we should not do anything that will endanger someone's life or stand idly by when we could save a life.

Suddenly this commandment is not so simple. It

opens up a huge moral can of worms, especially for us in affluent countries who routinely let people die whom we could save and, even more disturbingly, participate in systems that kill.

Killing versus Letting Die

We let people die every day, for reasons that are personal, political, cultural, and complicated. We ignore advertisements that explain how for some relatively small sum of money, we can save the life of a child in Bangladesh, or if we give—perhaps even a great deal—we're generally not spending every available cent to save these children. On a city street, we may pass a person lying in a heap and—especially if he "looks homeless"—keep walking, not knowing what will become of him.

In American culture we tend to assume a significant moral difference between killing and letting die. Western conventional ethics suggest that we have a negative obligation to not hurt others, but not a positive obligation to help others. We can go to prison for shooting someone but not for failing to warn someone that she is about to be shot. We have an obligation to not push someone who can't swim into a swimming pool but no obligation to rescue someone who can't swim and who is already drowning in that same pool.

Jewish ethics, on the other hand, entails positive obligations. We *are* obliged to warn someone who is in danger and to save a drowning person if we can do it without drowning ourselves. Perhaps the medieval rabbis, in their various interpretations of the sixth commandment, are contesting the idea that killing and letting die are really so different.

Modern-day philosopher James Rachels illustrates the argument this way:

A woman wants her uncle dead, and she gives him poison in his coffee. Another woman, who also wants her uncle dead, is about to give him poison when she sees him unknowingly drink poison from another source. She watches him die, withholding the antidote in her pocket. Does either woman behave better? If the bare difference between killing and letting die were morally important, then the second woman's behavior would be better. But it is not. Therefore, the argument goes, the difference between killing and letting die is not morally important.

But, some of us might protest, the woman in each case *wants* her uncle dead. Her murderous intention is the problem here, not whether she did or did not personally hand him the poisoned coffee. Intention does seem to matter. When we go out to dinner instead of sending the money to a starving child in Bangladesh, we don't *want* the child to die. As far as we are concerned, he is in another galaxy. Our decision to eat out has nothing to do with him. And while that makes an emotional difference to us, it makes no difference whatsoever to the Bangladeshi child. And it may make no difference from the standpoint of the sixth commandment either.

How Much We Love Our Bugatti

Ethicist Peter Singer takes up this very question. Is letting someone die, not because we want them to die but simply because we blithely indulge other priorities, tantamount to "killing"? And is it as ethically problematic? In his famous ethical dilemma, Singer describes a scenario where a man has just bought a brand-new, shiny Bugatti that is his pride and joy. His Bugatti is parked near a railroad track. A runaway train with no one aboard comes barreling down the line headed toward where some children are playing on the tracks. By throwing a switch, the man could redirect the train to a different track where it would miss hitting the children but crash into his Bugatti. But he loves his new car so much, he can't bring himself to throw the switch. He walks away, pretending he didn't see, and the children are killed.

Most of us would agree that the man's action is reprehensible, immoral, and just plain wrong. The fact that it is technically an *inaction* (he didn't kill them; he just passively let them die) matters little to the morality of his decision. Likewise, the fact that he didn't particularly *want* the children to die but rather was more concerned with preserving his car also matters little to the morality of his decision. We would condemn him in the strongest possible terms. And yet we in affluent countries are presented with this scenario every single day and every day we fail to throw the switch. Across the world there are millions of children right now who are essentially playing on the tracks, and we, for the sake of things like our cars, pretend we don't see and keep walking. We could save them, at least some of them, but we don't.

Over one billion people in this world live in extreme poverty. These people eat one meal a day at best, sometimes having to choose between feeding their children and feeding themselves. They live in an unstable house made of mud or thatch that they constantly have to rebuild when there's severe weather, which is more and more often these days. They are unable to save any money and have no backup if someone in the family needs to see a doctor or needs medicine. They have no safe drinking water nearby—they have to walk a long way for water, and even then, it will make a person sick unless it is boiled. Extreme poverty is more than just extremely unpleasant; it kills people, reliably. Millions of children die every year because of it.

According to the World Bank, it takes an income of something on the order of $1.25 a day to avoid such extreme poverty. Most middle-class and wealthy people spend much more than this each day on goods and services that are unarguably luxuries—a dinner out when one could probably prepare something at home, a new coat when one already has a coat, a professional haircut when one owns a pair of scissors. Instead of doing these things, we are free to give all the money we would have spent to organizations working in developing countries. We could be lifting people out of poverty, $1.25 at a time, without any fear that we ourselves would become poor. We are free to strip down to the bare essentials of life so that others can survive. But almost no one does this. We enjoy eating at restaurants too much, we feel gratified—even empowered—by a purchase of a new coat, we feel enormous social pressure to have a haircut that looks "normal." We love our Bugatti so much that we pretend we haven't seen the children playing in the tracks.

Systems that Kill

So perhaps in addition to refraining from murdering people, in order to keep the sixth commandment we need to give a much higher percentage of our money to charity. Maybe we need to give a 10 percent tithe or even more. Perhaps that would fulfill not only the "not killing" aspect but also the "not letting die" aspect of the law. But as it turns out, extreme poverty in the developing world is only the tips of the branches of a huge tree—it is only the end result of a vast economic and cultural system that has a life of its own. If everyone in affluent countries gave significantly more of our income to international aid and world hunger organizations, the tips of the branches would be clipped—maybe a generation of children could be saved. But if we do not change the underlying economic systems and the even more deeply underlying spiritual orientation, if we do not uproot the tree altogether, it will regrow. Poverty will regenerate and people will begin dying again as the systems dispassionately adjust to a new influx of cash.

The obligation to not kill goes deeper than charity. We live in an interconnected global society in which many of the products that we rely on in our daily lives are produced at the expense of the health and sometimes the lives of people far away. The strawberries we eat may be grown with pesticides that cause cancer and birth defects in the farmworkers and their families. The T-shirts we wear may be made by workers in factories that collapse. The burger we eat may be made from a cow who was fed grain grown on an industrial farm in Brazil where the local people are starving. The field of grain grown for cows is no longer available to grow food to feed humans. And the cow meat is too expensive for the locals to buy. These types of causal connections are complicated and often intentionally obscured by the cheerful branding of the products we buy. But the modern world has also produced a level of sophistication that should allow us to grasp what's going on. It is incumbent on us to learn, or else we are no better than Peter Singer's man by the tracks who looks away.

We're not talking about individuals, but systems that kill. If we understand *lo tirtzach* to include the systems *in which we participate*, then our noncontroversial commandment has suddenly become politically radical.

Contemporary theologians, including the current pope, are understanding it in exactly this way. In the apostolic exhortation he released in November 2013, Pope Francis wrote,

> Just as the commandment "Thou shalt not kill"
> sets a clear limit in order to safeguard the value of

human life, today we also have to say "thou shalt not" to an economy of exclusion and inequality. Such an economy kills. How can it be that it is not a news item when an elderly homeless person dies of exposure, but it is news when the stock market loses two points?...Can we continue to stand by when food is thrown away when people are starving?...Today everything comes under the laws of competition and the survival of the fittest, where the powerful feed upon the powerless. As a consequence, masses of people find themselves excluded and marginalized: without work, without possibilities, without any means of escape.

At the time that the Torah was written, no one could possibly have anticipated a world in which *systems* could kill; in which we could communicate with people we would never meet; where we could passively, inadvertently, indirectly kill people on the other side of the planet. *Lo tirtzach* asks the question, What are our religious obligations to others in a system that compounds individual actions and inactions? Conservative factions of our society generally refuse to engage this question. Conservatives prefer to identify individual bad actors. If someone kills a person directly, that is a sin, a violation of the sixth commandment, and must be punished.

But if hundreds, thousands, or millions die from mal-nutrition, poor health care, floods, droughts, or indus-trial chemical poisoning, the collective or corporate bad actors are not held accountable. Instead, the tragedy is chalked up to innocent human error, social or biologi-cal Darwinism, or "acts of God."

Waking Up in Flint

During the 2016 water crisis in Flint, Michigan, there was much political jockeying to avoid blame for the disaster of lead and other toxins winding up in the city's drinking water. Specifically, authorities sought to dismiss as a coincidence that the thousands of children and adults whose water was contaminated with lead were mostly black. Conservative talking points included an insistence that it's unfair to politicize the issue. There was a refusal to view the problem as a product of systemic injustice or environmental racism. One politician said, "I don't think someone woke up one morning and said let's figure out how to poison the water system to hurt someone."

He was absolutely right about that. Nobody did just wake up one morning and decide to hurt someone. Instead, someone, to save money, decided to unhook the city of Flint from its freshwater source, Lake Huron, and hook it up to the polluted Flint River. Someone else, to save money, decided to not treat the water with a chemical that would keep lead out of it. When the crisis began to come to light, someone ignored it, someone hid evidence, and someone tampered with lead tests, to save their own jobs. When people complained about the yellow, foul-tasting water, someone advised them to boil it, which of course does nothing to remediate lead. When General Motors complained that the water was corroding the car engines in their Flint plant, someone decided to switch them, *and only them*, back to Lake Huron water. Someone thought it was okay to let children drink water that corrodes engines.

No one wanted to hurt people, but all willingly participated in a system that hurt many people, especially children, and jeopardized lives. Perhaps this is because the lives jeopardized were, as is so often the case, lives of people of color. We hear the warnings of the rabbinic commentators in our ears again: "Do not murder, either physically or by your speech by lying, gossiping, [or] deliberately giving fatal advice." The bureaucrats and power players of Flint, Michigan, were not unique or even unusual in ignoring the systemic contexts of their actions. We all do it—some knowingly, some unknowingly, most of us somewhere in between, floating in a kind of willful ignorance. We choose to remain only dimly aware of things of which we should be keenly aware because lives are at stake. It's a spiritual failure in which we all participate. Capitalism itself—at least as it's practiced today in the United States—requires it.

We violate the sixth commandment for profit: Drug companies let people die rather than price drugs at a cost that's affordable. They fiercely guard the intellectual property of these drugs, a clear instance of what Rabbi Ibn Ezra called "failing to reveal a secret that might save a life." When employees at an automaker become aware that they are sending vehicles out into the marketplace that have faulty parts that can and have caused deaths and don't speak up about it, it is an instance of what Rabbi Hizkuni called "remaining silent when a murderer's plans become known to you." Murder, of course, is not the intention. But again, what difference does it make to the victims whether their deaths are caused by hostility or by indifference?

Vandalizing Creation

Nowhere is this mass silence around the workings of systems more pervasive or more lethal than it is around the systems currently propelling ecological collapse and climate change. The US economy is substantially contributing to an overheating planet, causing deadly storms, droughts, and rising waters that have killed many and will kill many more. Our corporations control ever greater percentages of the earth's freshwater, profiting from its profligate use in industry and amassing huge wealth bottling it and selling it as a "safer" and more convenient alternative to tap water. Meanwhile over one billion people in the world lack access to safe drinking water and the World Bank has predicted that in the next decade two-thirds of the earth's people will face a water shortage. This too spells death. The list goes on and on of the ways in which our systems result in collective violations of the commandment *lo tirtzach*.

Just as in the case of the Flint water crisis, few of us, including the vast majority of corporate executives, are waking up in the morning and setting out to hurt anyone. Some of us are unaware that systemic violence exists, although the majority of middle-class and wealthy people in affluent countries are aware, at least vaguely. But we struggle to get through the day, do our jobs, survive discrimination, or get food on the table for our kids, and such seemingly distant concerns cannot rise to the surface of our consciousness. The consequences to our lives of a full reckoning with the truth would be too disruptive or perhaps the guilt of our complicity would be overwhelming. We pretend to not know what we know and we try not to know too much. We bury our head in the sand to escape the unwanted signs of danger—a move that, as it turns out, even ostriches are too wise to make.

Killing Other Animals

In the biblical seven-day Creation myth, all land animals, including humans, are created together on the sixth day. This is positioned as the culminating act of creation and this creative act, unlike all the others, is accompanied by some instructions. God says to the first human, "I have given you every plant yielding seed that is upon the face of all the earth, and every tree with seed in its fruit; you shall have them for food." Full stop. The glaring omission on the menu here, of course, is animals. In this story, the first humans were supposed to be vegan. Animals were not food.

Fast-forward to the Genesis flood story in which the text actually says that God regrets having made humans because of their violence. In the narrative, when finally the rain stops and the waters recede, God brings the goal posts in a little closer with a new set of instructions called the Noahide Laws. God tells Noah that from now on, humans can kill certain animals for food but may not kill other humans. And, with the sign of the rainbow, God promises to never destroy the earth by flood again (Genesis 9). There is a sweetness to this ending in that God now sees human nature and accepts humans as they are. Yet it is clearly a fallen state. There remains a lingering sense that everything would have been better if humans had just been able to stick with the program in the first place.

What eating animals has become today, the way it has impacted this planet, the people in the ancient Near East could not have envisioned in their wildest dreams. It is fundamentally changing the nature of the physical world described in that Creation story. Animal agriculture as an industry is responsible for at least a quarter of the world's greenhouse gas emissions and massive deforestation, which makes it the biggest contributor to global warming. It uses massive quantities of water. It takes 2,500 gallons of water to produce one pound of beef. Animal agriculture is the leading cause of species extinction, ocean dead zones, and water pollution. The skies and the seas, the grasses and trees, the delicate interwoven systems of life are being damaged by humans violating that very first boundary on our power.

All of this translates to human deaths—some already today in the form of people killed by drought and extreme weather, farmworkers getting cancer from exposure to agrochemicals, epidemics of obesity and heart disease. Experts predict that climate change and environmental degradation will be responsible for widespread famine and force millions to become refugees, resulting in global destabilization and war. And yet a veil of silence covers this entire arena of inquiry. Most people, most politicians, even most environmental organizations refuse to talk about the environmental impact of animal agriculture, because the political cost of raising the topic is too great.

Religious Veganism

It is a logical conclusion that one way to keep the commandment against killing would be to eat an entirely plant-based diet—to refuse to participate in this system that kills so many and will kill so many more. But for many of us, as for the mythical early humans in Genesis, this is prohibitively difficult. We love our pizza and our chicken and our ground-beef tacos. The foods produced through animal agriculture are so beloved and such a part of Western culture, to question it is literally unthinkable. The animals involved are euphemistically called "livestock"—units of product (stock) that happen to be alive. The easy-to-keep commandment, understood this way, has turned into a huge challenge.

Take ice cream. We think of ice cream as a cold treat that comes in many colors and flavors, with or without sprinkles (don't ask what a "sprinkle" is made of), with or without chocolate chips (don't ask where the chocolate comes from). Ice cream is a ritual of childhood and adulthood; it's sold from trucks in the summer; entire pints may be consumed solo after a breakup. Ice cream, as we know it, is completely removed from what it actually is: warm milk from a mother cow, intended by nature for feeding her calves. We don't know what kind of life the particular cow leads who made the milk for any given cookie dough ice cream on a waffle cone. We can guess that it's not pretty.

But we dare not think about that. Nor dare we think about the rain forest that was cut down to grow feed for that cow; nor the people living in and near that rain forest who had previously relied on it for sustenance; nor the carbon that will now not be sequestered by the green plants of that rain forest, accelerating global warming; nor the workers who may have grown ill from handling the pesticides used to grow the feed; nor the massive amount of water used to produce that one scoop of ice cream in a world where people are dying from thirst. We dare not think that when we eat animal products, not only are we killing animals, but we are fueling systems that kill humans.

Active Nonviolence

One of the frustrations of a systemic reading of *lo tirtzach* is that, while we could fully discharge our obligation to not kill in the commandment's original context, it is virtually impossible today. If we set out to not let anyone die, we could devote our whole lives to it and still we would fail. Even if we kill no one directly with malicious intent, eat a vegan diet, tithe to world hunger organizations, buy all fair-trade products, and make every effort to be "good" in every way, our very participation in the culture of an affluent society implicates us in the deaths of others. (Watching a movie, for example, supports an industry that generates massive amounts of waste and more air pollution than almost any other industry.) So what is the religious obligation of this commandment when our best efforts to keep it would be doomed to failure?

New Zealand bishops, in a Catholic statement on the environment, pose this very question:

> What does the commandment *"Thou shall not kill"* mean when twenty percent of the world's population consumes resources at a rate that robs poorer nations and future generations of what they need to survive? What does it mean to respect life when 30,000 people die each day from poverty? What does it mean to be stewards of the earth when up to half of all living species are expected to become extinct in the next 200 years? ... Our world is facing an ecological crisis,

which could equally be called an economic crisis, or a poverty crisis. Its public face is the suffering of the poor and the degradation of our environment, at a time when accumulation of wealth and material goods has never occupied our attention more. That is why we see it primarily as a spiritual or moral crisis.

We are enacting a collective violation of the sixth commandment. It is hard to know whether the "accumulation of wealth and material goods has never occupied our attention more" than it does today; the Ten Commandments seem to have been written to resist and counter exactly such a preoccupation in the ancient world. But the bishops' declaration is important because it frames the issue as a spiritual crisis. That we all participate in systems that kill exposes a culture and an economy that are spiritually bereft. This commandment calls us to a spiritually grounded resistance to that culture and that economy at their roots, challenging all of the assumptions of contemporary capitalism that result in the deaths of others.

Boots on the Ground

The sixth commandment calls us on a spiritual level to embrace our siblinghood with all of humanity and with all creatures of the earth. We are called to a genuine accountability to others—be our siblings' keeper, even those far away—and to take some responsibility for their welfare. We are called to cherish the worth of their lives through our actions, even if it means—and it will—that we inconvenience ourselves, push out beyond our comfort zones, and make real sacrifices in the way we live our lives.

This kind of elevated spiritual consciousness can manifest itself in many ways, consumer choices being only one. But to be faithful to this commandment is, in one way or another, to have boots on the ground. It means actively working to build a spiritually grounded culture and economy that support life.

A spiritual grounding for this work might lead us to oppose military spending and redirect public funds to social safety nets or foreign aid. It might inspire us to become active in the Movement for Black Lives, promoting community-based policing and anti-racism work. It might inspire us to become doctors or nurses working in underserved communities. It might move us to lobby for stricter gun laws, antipoverty initiatives, and expanded Medicare and Medicaid. It might inspire us to work for environmental sustainability on behalf of all lives, present and future.

An elevated consciousness will deflate the perceived

importance of maintaining our comforts and align us with a larger sense of connection with the divine in each person. On a cultural level, it will call us to create different kinds of institutions—ones that gauge their success on the basis of how much compassion and health and community are created by their activities, not how much money and power.

This sixth commandment, which cannot fully be kept individually in the current social order, can be kept collectively through a common spiritual revolution. It serves as a north star—an orientation toward the world to which we should all aspire. As we seek to transform society, we can use this commandment—and all the commandments—as a measure of our progress. We can seek to understand it as Nachmanides understood it—that we are not to vandalize creation by spilling human blood. We are not to vandalize creation at all. The world with all its creatures is a living work of art in which every brush stroke is crucial. The commandment "Do not kill" calls us as religious people to nurture life on this earth, to support systems that are healthy and compassionate, to speak up when we see lethal injustice. "Do not kill" at its simplest is a call for world peace: a call for each of us to protect, honor, and serve all the creatures of the earth.

LO TINAF

▼

The Seventh Commandment

Do Not Commit Adultery

▲

Stay In for the Long Run,
Reject Throwaway Culture

Do not commit adultery.

Public judgment about what goes on in private bedrooms gets our hackles up. Modern people tend to value privacy and conscience and we increasingly include a wide range of sexual practices in the big tent of okay-ness. The word "adultery" itself seems to lift a relationship out of the private sphere and inappropriately transfer it to the public sphere. Does a commandment about whom you "shalt" and "shalt not" have sex with have any place at all in our contemporary world?

One rationale used to explain the ancient prohibition against adultery is the practical goal of being able to keep track of whose children are whose. In the ancient Near East, you had to know who your daddy was because important inheritances like land and blessings flowed through the paternal line. Now that we have wills and laws governing estates, and DNA testing to determine paternity, it may appear that the seventh commandment is merely a vestigial limb of a patriarchal era.

Because our public discussions are rife with sexual politics, it's first important to note that, judging from the rabbinic commentaries, the scope of the seventh commandment is narrow. It seems that the prohibition *lo tinaf*:

- refers to having sex with a person other than the person you're married to or having sex with someone who is married to someone other than you
- applies equally to women and men
- does not refer to premarital sex
- is not a prohibition against any particular sex acts or sexual pleasure
- probably assumes a heterosexual marriage but nowhere explicitly states what kinds of marriages do or don't "count"

The commandment is solely a prohibition against breaking a marriage covenant.

Pro-sex, Pro-commitment

The Talmud (the body of rabbinic writings that interpret the Hebrew Bible) contains extremely progressive and sex-positive teachings, certainly for its era and even by today's standards. Within marriage, sex is celebrated as a gift from God and is a mitzvah (a virtuous practice or commandment) even when the couple is beyond childbearing age. Popular culture gives the impression that biblical traditions on sex are prudish or that sex is a necessary evil to be used only for procreation, but that is not true.

According to these ancient teachings, a husband may not force his wife to have sex. Sex is a marital right that the wife specifically is entitled to. A woman can divorce her husband if he doesn't have enough sex with her, even if they already have children. A woman can divorce her husband if he doesn't give her sexual pleasure. Rules are provided for how often the husband must offer his wife sex: if he is independently wealthy and not working, it's every day; if he's a day laborer, it's twice a week; if he's a donkey driver, it's once a week; if he's a camel driver, it's once a month; and if he's a sailor, it's once every six months. Further, if the husband has the option, he should choose an occupation that allows him to be available to his wife for sex more often (say, donkey driving) even if a different job (say, camel driving) would pay more but would make him less available.

As for what exactly a couple is permitted to do in bed: after a long, explicit discussion of various options, the Talmud concludes, "In the final analysis, a husband and wife can do whatever pleases them most."

This makes the seventh commandment less about sexual activity and more about covenant—commitment. Two people are in a relationship, have made commitments to one another, and are required to keep those commitments. This commandment gets at the heart of what it means to be in relationship, to keep commitments even when one would rather not, to devote oneself to something flawed, to love someone imperfect, to work at something when it's hard, and to stop shopping for something better.

The implications of the seventh commandment go beyond patriarchal lineage customs, even beyond contemporary nuclear family ideals and the social stability that supposedly ensues. It is not justification for any side of the argument about whether the two-parent family is the best kind for children, for adults, and for society as a whole. It is about something deeper.

Loyalty to something imperfect is almost foreign to us today. Under corporate capitalism, we are expected to trade in and trade up our goods and services at every opportunity. Repairing something broken is also foreign. We are expected to buy a new one instead. People, too, are to be valued for their attractiveness and usefulness and discarded when those qualities fade. This commandment challenges us to de-commodify and re-enchant the people in our lives.

Dating and Other Transactions

Childhood and youth often include built-in community; we may go to a school in or near our neighborhood; we see the same kids every day for years in classes and then again in playgrounds and basketball courts, and sometimes again at religious services. Our relationships are what sociologists call "multistranded." If and when we start forming romantic connections, they are with people we know. Those fortunate enough to go to college enjoy a brief extension of this feeling of connectedness. For many of us, it is the last environment in which we may live and work enmeshed with a community of people who share similar cultural expectations, ages, and life stages. College can feel like our last best hope of finding a life partner.

After that our social worlds become less organic. A single adult may have work colleagues and maybe some remaining friends from high school or college, but probably no built-in communities and few multistranded relationships. The different arenas of our lives can be walled off from each other. In this context, finding a life partner can be extraordinarily difficult. When we have romantic interest in someone, it is generally not someone we have known from childhood. He or she is a stranger. Getting to know this person isn't deepening a preexisting relationship; instead it is testing out a brand-new one. We learn about someone from the outside in. We evaluate the other person according to multiple criteria ranging from physical attractiveness to life goals to faith to personal qualities. We ask ourselves, "Is this someone I could fall in love with?" And we are acutely aware of being evaluated in the same ways. This evaluation process is called dating.

Dating—through parties, bars, setups, hookups, websites, and apps—helps compensate for the isolation of contemporary American adulthood. It is an adaptation of modern life and it carries with it the telltale stamp of our era: commodification. Necessary as it may be for many of us, dating is a pale imitation of the more natural ways of forming relationships. Consider the world of online dating: people are flattened, marketed, and displayed like products. The "shopper" browses the catalog. He or she has no option but to rank these two-dimensional packaged, branded constructions. The courtship becomes transactional. The most empowering advice people sometimes get while enduring this modern ritual is "Remember, honey, *you're* the buyer." While many good relationships and marriages have begun in just this way, the process is inherently dehumanizing.

This process would have been completely alien to

any human societies before a hundred years ago and certainly in the days of the writing of the Ten Commandments. Marriages were arranged by parents, specifically fathers, between members of the same community. The weddings were joyful, not because true love had been found and realized, but because a domestic unit of stability had been formed to stave off hunger and the dangers of an uncertain life. One didn't "choose" one's spouse any more than one chose one's parents or children. The spouse was family, and as with any family, as they say, "When you have to go there, they have to take you in."

Choosing and Unchoosing

Sholem Rabinovich's 1894 series of stories about Tevye the milkman chronicles Tevye's struggles with the changing meanings of marriage, as novel notions of "love" and "attraction" enter his small shtetl in czarist Russia. In *Fiddler on the Roof,* Tevye and his wife, Golde, sing a poignant song in which Tevye famously asks her, "Do you love me?" The question does not compute. She had never thought to evaluate their relationship in those terms. She can only reply in terms of the devotion and commitment that she had practiced through her unglamorous hard work for twenty-five years—the cooking and the laundry, raising children, and milking the cow. By the end of the song, they decide that the life they have built together and the ups and downs they have shared, including starvation, cumulatively constitute love. And so, in fact, they suppose they love one another. In a sweet ending to "Do You Love Me?" they claim a place for "love" in a relationship without "choice."

The rest of the world moves on without them, however, both in the fiction story and in reality. We have now arrived at the polar opposite of that world of the Russian shtetl. Old world hierarchies have given way to what is touted as a more horizontal world of freedom. Now, not only do we arrange our own marriages, choosing according to our own—often highly impractical—criteria, but we feel free to continue choosing once married. Couples will speak the words "for as long as we both shall live" while simultaneously signing prenuptial agreements. Divorce is common and acceptable, and some significant percentage of married people commit adultery. If you can choose something, you can always unchoose it.

In a culture of choosing and unchoosing one's spouse, the lessons of the retail marketplace carry over: the appraisal phase never really ends. People view and evaluate one another the way we view and evaluate commodities. Even once we're married, the galaxy of other potential mates still sparkles on the horizon. Other people's spouses still feel, at least in theory, accessible. The ongoing availability of choice is construed as power in our culture: the more successful we are, the more choice we have. In commerce we exercise that choice by buying a second or third television; in marriage, by committing adultery.

Our participation in consumer culture has taught us to center our own desires in decision-making of all kinds. We understand the pursuit of happiness to be an "inalienable right" and our happiness to hinge on getting what we want. We may not always *succeed* in getting what we want, but we have the unfettered right to try. In the realm of marriage, this means that nothing should interfere with our pursuing an adulterous affair except our feelings of love for our spouse (which is really just a different "want" competing for fulfillment). In the realm of commerce, it means that nothing external should constrain our ability to buy anything, sell anything, use any quantity of resources (water, energy, trees) if such use can be defended in terms of the pursuit of happiness and our freedom of choice.

Worshipping a Human Idol

Rabbinic commentators have noted that the Ten Commandments can be read not only down but *across* the two tablets. Each commandment having to do with our relationship with God on the first tablet has a corresponding one having to do with our relationship with humans on the second tablet.

1. No Other Gods besides Me	6. Do Not Kill
2. Worship No Images	7. Do Not Commit Adultery
3. Do Not Take God's Name in Vain	8. Do Not Steal
4. Observe the Sabbath	9. Do Not Lie
5. Honor Your Father and Your Mother	10. Do Not Covet

In the case of *lo tinaf*, the corresponding commandment is the second commandment—the one prohibiting us from making a *t'munah* and bowing down and serving it. It's the prohibition against idol worship. When we worship an idol, we invest something artificial with the power of the real. We locate our faith and loyalty in something false. There's an obvious parallel here to having an affair. In a relationship in which a couple has promised sexual exclusivity, the partner or spouse is the "real" God and the outside lover is the idol. Adultery is investing an outside relationship with the intimacy and attention that we have promised to reserve for our partner.

We commit adultery for the same reasons we serve other idols—we believe wrongly that by investing ourselves in another person or object or goal that we will finally get the ineffable powers that we're looking for. There are biological drivers for infidelity as well, but in many cases the motivation to violate such a fundamental trust runs much deeper. Perhaps by having sex with someone else, we can feel vital and desirable in a way that we don't feel with our spouse. Perhaps we can feel affirmed and respected in a way that we don't feel at work. Perhaps we can feel some relief from the crushing pressure of paying the rent and grocery bills. Perhaps we can feel that ineffable sense of wholeness. Perhaps we can feel childlike wonder at the discovery of another human being—that intoxicating, giddy rush of first love. Perhaps we are terrified of the inexorable process of growing older, watching our life options fade away, seeing one door after another slam shut. We can see that the end of this road is death. With someone else, perhaps we can briefly feel immortal.

The primary partner can never compete with someone new on the level of pure appeal. Like the golden calf, another hot woman's or man's body is enticing in its glittery simplicity. It promises to fulfill our needs and we reach for it. The relationship with the extramarital lover has no baggage; it is unencumbered by the hard work of commitment and compromise. It offers the illusion of freedom. In the new, temporary, unencumbered relationship we can be free to be who we want to be. The lover is a projection of our yearnings and can be whatever we yearn for. He or she is, in this sense, an illusion—shimmering, two-dimensional, and utterly insubstantial; something we make with our own hands, like the golden calf, and then proceed to worship.

Real relationships are demanding and marbled, complicated and imperfect. Anyone who has been in a long-term relationship knows that it's hard to keep the fires of passion burning while doing the mundane work of building a life together—cooking the meals, doing the laundry...milking the cow. This is why books like *Mating in Captivity* (about marriage) and *All Joy and No Fun* (about kids) are so popular. And the temptation to infidelity is even greater if there are serious problems in the relationship.

Adultery Doesn't Work

The problem is that we rarely get what we want out of adultery. (Unless what we want is to explode the marriage.) Vitality, freedom, personal power, sexual energy, and enchantment with life are spiritual and psychological capacities. They can only come from God and from deep within. Ultimately if we're with a new person or our spouse, we're still going to be with ourselves. We bring to either relationship our gifts, wounds, and needs. And any other person brings their gifts, wounds, and needs. The result is another messy and imperfect relationship. We go out searching for love, trying to fill some need, scratch some itch, cure some ennui. It's "going to the hardware store to look for a gallon of milk," looking for something where we're not going to find it. Except in the rarest of instances, what we seek simply isn't going to be there. We can make offerings to the golden calf all we want, but the rain isn't going to fall and water the parched earth.

In some cases, a marriage is truly bad—unhealthy, unsafe, or genuinely failing to meet legitimate relationship needs. But in such cases, adultery is—let's be honest—a cowardly way out. It betrays an unwillingness to face truth, have tough conversations, face change or loneliness. Another relationship might in fact be better, but through marital infidelity, we have invoked a swirling morass of drama in our lives. Depending on the circumstances, we may have lied and maintained secret online accounts, spent time and energy orchestrating furtive rendezvous, or devoted years of our emotional energy to the attendant questions, problems, and fantasies. We may have lost the esteem of others, hurt our spouse (whom we may still love), and hurt children. To do all of this is to make very real sacrifices of time, money, and the delicate trust of intimate relationships— sacrificial offerings for the worship of an idol.

Dignity

The commandment prohibiting adultery requires us to cultivate dignity. It teaches us to take our own lives seriously and not fritter them away sending secret text messages, scrambling to satisfy momentary desires, and chasing illusions. It teaches us to take pride in our lives, choices, and relationships, even though they are flawed. It teaches us to live with integrity, keep our word, and earn the trust of those around us. This leads to a richer and more meaningful life.

Adultery can be a double-edged sword. It harms the victim (the spouse who is betrayed), but it can also be spiritually disastrous for the one who commits the act. Accounts of people who have committed adultery reveal that it diminishes dignity and self-respect. Many claim a loss of agency. A man describes having been seduced at a bar where he knew he shouldn't have gone. A woman describes not having wanted or expected to wind up having sex with another man, but somehow it happened anyway. A one-time fling became a secret compulsion that went on for months or years. In adultery, we dodge accountability, feel ourselves in the grip of uncontainable desire or overwhelmed by something larger than ourselves. This recalls idol worship—we give up our power to a false god. To the extent that we relinquish responsibility, we become alienated from ourselves ("I don't know what happened; I just threw my gold jewelry into the fire and out popped this calf!").

If we can't be held accountable for whom we do and don't have sex with, for what can we be held accountable? If we allow ourselves to write off our actions in this area and violate a sacred trust because of ostensibly uncontrollable desires, how much easier it must be to accept desire as cover for our behavior in other areas of life, where it feels like less is at stake. Capitulation of our will does not stay confined to one area. We become weaker, less spine-full people who can't even trust ourselves to make the decisions we decide to make.

To keep this commandment is to claim that we do have the power of choice—we can determine the kind of people we want to be and the kind of lives we want to lead. It is to claim free will—the foundation of our participation as citizens in the social contract and our birthright as spiritual beings.

Protecting Innocence

Dignity is further undermined by adultery when the dishonesty of the act metastasizes, as it frequently does, and upends the whole project. One woman tells a story of her affair with a man who would have wild sex with her and text her love notes all day long. She had bought a cheap cell phone that she only kept at work for the purposes of texting with her lover. She would make up lie after lie to explain to her husband why she was coming home late time and again. This went on for years—her lover professing his undying love, claiming that she was the one. And then suddenly, after a day of flowery missives like any other day, he broke up with her by text. He explained that he felt overwrought with guilt and the only way to purge his guilt was to end his affair with her. She was devastated. Things got worse when she looked at Facebook the next day and found that he was overjoyed to be labeling himself as "in a relationship"...with someone else. She realized that this was not a brand-new relationship. While she had been cheating on her husband, her lover had been cheating on her. Dishonesty tends to boomerang back and infect every area of one's life.

Finally, it is difficult to feel a sense of personal dignity when we know we have chased an idol at the expense of someone we loved. Lies and secrets rarely stay hidden forever. In some unforeseeable, mysterious way, adultery often gets discovered. And when our infidelity comes to light, we have to face the knowledge that we did something that had a high chance of resulting in spiritual trauma for our spouse.

Adultery tends to destroy a person's trust, not only in the adulterer, but in life in general. People whose partners have been unfaithful will describe feeling as if the ground had shifted under them. Everything that they thought was true about life gets called into question. Everyone they previously trusted is now regarded with suspicion. They feel unsafe. And the promise of true love, rhapsodized in our culture, is shattered by the very person in whom they had invested that most intimate hope. They can experience a loss of innocence that can never be recovered. And we, the adulterer, will know for the rest of our lives that we needed that idol so badly, we were willing to risk anything, including the innocence of our partner, to get it.

On a spiritual level, keeping this seventh commandment is a powerful tool for protecting innocence in the world. As we have seen in exploring the third commandment on taking the name of YHVH in vain, the protection of innocence is not a trivial thing. It has profound and far-reaching consequences. At stake is our faith not only in God but in one another and all our social institutions. When that faith has been shattered, when we have been lied to and betrayed by our most intimate partners, the world feels more dangerous and we respond from a defensive position. We face life embattled, taking care of ourselves first and foremost, and supporting public policies that protect us from others. Conversely, when people trust one another and feel fundamentally safe, we are much better able to access our own compassion for others and support public policies of openhearted generosity. We naturally create a culture based on love.

Stopping Shopping

The notion of disposability is built into American culture. Planned obsolescence is a time-honored business practice. Even the liberals among us often accept single-use items for convenience and habit—taking a plastic bag to carry one item and then throwing it away five minutes later; bringing paper plates and plastic cups to a kid's school party and then throwing them away an hour later. There is a sense that the world is endlessly available to us for our casual use and that our convenience and desires are primary. Along with this comes the notion that newer is better. Buying new stuff every day is what it means to be an American. We never stop shopping. We take resources from the earth, process them through human labor and the use of more natural resources, sell and buy them, use them for a period of time, and then discard them, usually into a landfill where the elements that comprise them will never again return to the life cycle of the earth.

Each one of us ages, develops lined faces and sagging bodies. Our energy flags, our eyesight dims, we are less able to do the things we love as we get older. From a biological standpoint, there is no use for a human after childbearing years; our bodies begin a slow decline. As this process unfolds, adultery becomes more and more tempting. The same ethic we apply to products—that of choosing, using, and discarding—applies to people, even people with whom we have entered a sacred covenant. We are raised to believe that we are entitled to the fulfillment of our desires in every arena—that getting what we want will make us happy, and that we "deserve it." We don't really stop shopping...for anything.

The seventh commandment is countercultural because it teaches us to stop shopping. It teaches us to commit to what we have instead of scanning the horizon for something better. It teaches us to repair relationships when they are broken (and maybe we will learn from this to repair toasters when they are broken). It challenges us to remain in relationship with someone or something imperfect; to stay faithful to a person even when he or she is outstripped by newer models; to see our partner not as a commodity but as an irreducible human miracle.

When we do this, it forces us to look harder at ourselves. Instead of seeking spiritual powers in the extramarital lover or the new shoes or handheld device, we have to seek them in the power of YHVH within. We relinquish our other gods. This, in turn, creates a life of greater dignity, honesty, and integrity. This dignity, honesty, and integrity ripple out and create webs of relationships that are more trusting and compassionate. Keeping the commandment *lo tinaf* does not guarantee that one will live a good, rich, and meaningful life, or that the world will become more whole, but it is one of the practices that creates the conditions of possibility for it.

LO TIGNOV

▼

The Eighth Commandment

Do Not Steal

▲

*Pay What Stuff Really
Costs in Fair Wages and the
Planet's Resources*

Do not steal.

If you want to climb Mount Everest, you have a small but real chance of dying. Along with the physical risks of falling into a crevasse or being buried in an avalanche, there are physiological risks—fatal conditions that you can acquire simply from exercising hard at such high altitudes. Human bodies weren't designed to do that. You need so much gear that you can't carry it all at once, and so you have to do laps, going up and back down and coming back up with more stuff. With each lap, you incur more risk. And so Western climbers who want to stand "on top of the world" talk a lot about risk-mitigation strategies. Chief among these strategies is hiring a Sherpa.

The Sherpa carries your stuff. The Sherpa—whose body was also not designed for this—does the laps up and down and back up again carrying heavy backpacks full of gear. You, meanwhile, do a single trip, carrying a backpack that looks big and full for the photos but that is packed with virtually nothing. At the end, the greatest share of the physical wear and tear and risk belongs to the Sherpa and the greatest share of the glory belongs to you. Working as a Sherpa in Nepal is one of the most dangerous jobs in the world. It's more dangerous than any nonmilitary job in the United States. Safety nets in this line of work are almost nonexistent. When a Sherpa dies, his family usually winds up impoverished with very little compensation from the guide company.

Does the commandment "Do not steal" (in Hebrew, *lo tignov*) have any relevance in hiring Sherpas? No one is stealing; the Sherpa is being paid. It is his choice, after all, to do this job and take this risk. By Western standards, the risk is not worth the money. That's why climbers are willing to pay the money to off-load the risk.

In today's global economy, the notion of stealing is layered and complicated in a way that it probably wasn't in biblical times. Back then, you could steal a goat or clothing or jewelry but not music or movies or the design of shredded wheat. You couldn't steal from an employee benefit plan, swindle investors through a Ponzi scheme, or pilfer from the government through tax evasion. To interpret the eighth commandment today requires a more nuanced understanding of what it means to take something that belongs to someone else.

Three Kinds of Theft

We steal in many ways and for many reasons. Some of us steal in the *old-fashioned way*. We cannot afford the things that we want or perhaps even need and we take someone else's. We don't believe, based on experience, that hard work will pan out for us. Perhaps we've seen our parents work hard for their whole lives with not much materially to show for it. If we steal a cell phone, we can turn it into cash on the black market within an hour at the local mobile store.

The middle class and wealthy steal, too, even without the motivation of financial need. White-collar crimes like embezzling, scams, and fraud fall into this category as does pirating music and cheating on one's taxes (as distinct from a principled refusal to pay). This *second way to steal* raises the question, Why would somebody of financial means steal? Theft to become even more wealthy or simply to get something small for "free" is a deeply spiritual matter.

We are embedded in a culture where we don't know one another and can imagine that the crime will not hurt any real person. The forest of economic, technological, and social forces around us is so dense, we can only see the trees—or the people—right in front of us. The person who steals a cell phone doesn't know the man who owned it, nor that the photos on it were invaluable, nor that he can't afford to buy a replacement. The white-collar criminal who defrauds investors doesn't know the woman who will lose her life savings in old age, be forced to sell her home, and live the rest of her days in poverty. The ethic of our culture is, it's everyone for oneself; do whatever you can get away with. In this sense, the poor, middle class, and rich all commit theft under the shadow of the same spiritual malady: alienation from others.

Nowhere is this kind of alienation more striking than in our daily consumer practices. Because we are insulated from the humans at the end of effect chains, supply chains, and food chains, we rarely, in this country, pay a fair-trade price for anything. A product's fair-trade price is a price that covers a living wage for all the workers who participated in making it; pays the cost of sustainably disposing of or recycling all the waste generated by its production; and provides for full replenishment of all natural resources impacted and extracted in the process. (There is no such thing as a fair-trade price for production that causes irreparable environmental damage, for example, causing the extinction of a species or the clear-cutting of a rain forest.)

We pay artificially deflated prices—$2.49 for a fast-food hamburger—when, if the workers were paid appropriately and the environmental impacts were sustainably offset and compensated for, the price would be astronomically higher. We may assume that by assiduously paying the listed market price, we are keeping the eighth commandment. But in our complex and interconnected global economy, the market price lies. Paying that price often amounts to a *third kind of stealing: systemic theft*.

The monetary difference between what we pay for something and its fair-trade price is the sum we steal.

Systemic Theft

Workers can never be paid the exact value of what they produce or there would be no profit margin for the business owner. Karl Marx explains that in a capitalist economy, workers must always generate "surplus value"—a market value that exceeds the cost of the workers' wages. A high surplus value indicates that something of value was produced for too little payment to the worker who produced it. A low surplus value suggests more equity. When the numbers from many workers are aggregated, surplus value can serve as a rough index of the balance of power between classes in a society. Today in the United States the average CEO makes a salary several hundred times that of the average worker.

The free market response to this might be that if a worker is not happy with his pay, he is free to find another job. An unskilled worker probably cannot find a better-paying job, but whether or not the worker could find another job—or is happy with his pay—is irrelevant from an ethical and religious standpoint. Employers routinely steal from employees by paying only a fraction of what their work is worth.

We know that if we stiff a worker for a day's wages, we have stolen from her. If we pay her twenty-five cents for the day's work, we have also stolen from her because although twenty-five cents is technically "pay," it's negligible and ethically no different from paying nothing. The stealing is clear. But it becomes complicated when we begin to determine how much we need to pay in order to *not* steal from her.

Consider the manufacture of pom-pom puffballs—the fuzzy accessories that attach to a purse or backpack. Some of them cost as much as $95 or more because they are marketed as luxury items made from real rabbit fur from China. (It's hard to know why someone would want this thing dangling from their bag, but such are the florid deformities of our consumer culture.) The factory worker is probably paid minimum wage. The employer can easily pay that wage and (subtracting for the rabbit fur, other materials, marketing, distribution, and depreciation and repairs on the puffball-making machinery), at $95 a pop, walk away with a massive profit. The extreme differential between the value the worker creates and the pay she receives suggests high surplus value. In other words, she is not paid fully for her work. In other words, she is stolen from.

Meanwhile the owner of the rabbit farm charges the factory owner only $1.70 per rabbit pelt. To keep his price so low, he has to externalize the massive environmental costs of animal agriculture. And he has to run his farm in a way that necessitates suffering on the part of the Chinese farm laborer who subsists on a pittance and on the part of the rabbit who lives in abhorrent conditions and then loses its life, quite literally, for nothing.

Systemic theft is complicated to unravel. If our goal is to individually and collectively keep the eighth commandment and "not steal," we have to acknowledge that through our consumer practices we often participate in grand larceny. We vote with our wallets, supporting and promoting stealing, even if we never directly steal ourselves. Having acknowledged this, how much *should* we pay for a product? How much *should* a worker get paid for manufacturing it? And how much *should* a corporation pay for whatever kind of "pelt" is taken from the natural world?

Treating People as Ends in Themselves

No financial formula can answer these questions. If it could, the solutions would be found in business or economics, but not religion. This kind of stealing, this systemic theft, is ultimately a spiritual question about how we relate to one another. The question is, Are we or are we not our siblings' keepers?

In the interpretive tradition of the Ten Commandments, we are given a clue to understand this obligation of not stealing in yet another way. The original meaning of the Hebrew verb *tignov*, translated as "steal," includes not only stealing generally, but also stealing a person: kidnapping. Kidnapping still happens today in the form of human trafficking, and working to end trafficking is a powerful way to observe this commandment. Most of us would never dream of participating in human trafficking, kidnapping, or stealing a person. But if we look more deeply at what it means to steal a person, the commandment is addressed to all of us.

Rabbi Naftali Silberberg of the Rohr Jewish Learning Institute says about this commandment, "The essence of kidnapping is utilizing another for personal gain." Kidnapping is objectifying and monetizing a person, commodifying the person for our own benefit. The commandment "Do not steal" could be restated as

Immanuel Kant's famous formula: "Always recognize that human individuals are ends, and do not use them as mere means to your end."

We might never physically kidnap someone, but fail to recognize people as ends in themselves? Use them as means to our ends? *That* we do. Like the Western climbers who hire Nepali Sherpas, we use other people to carry our stuff.

Stealing isn't only material or systemic. Romantic relationships maintained for the status the other person can convey through looks, power, money, class, or prestige is another kind of theft. The thief in such a relationship is always ready to "trade up." In the professional world we sometimes use others for personal gain; we cultivate friendships insofar as they are financially pragmatic and good for business, getting what we can out of the other person—the connections, the assistance, the free work, the sweet deal. Sometimes we see a teacher, therapist, clergy person, or parent as a means to get something we want rather than as a person. Those of us who are parents sometimes use our children for personal gain; we want them to act in a particular way or excel in particular areas because their behavior will reflect well on us. Or we use them as ammunition in a war with their other parent. Or we use their need for us to feed our ego and give us a sense of self-worth.

We all relate in these ways to some extent; it's just part of life. We use each other to get our needs met. We all use each other as "means" to various goals. Nothing is wrong with this as long as it's mutual, consensual, everyone's honest, and, most important, as long as that's not *all* that's going on. Kant's formula says we should not use people as *mere* means, but *also* treat them as ends in themselves. In other words, we shouldn't think *only* in terms of what others can do for us but strive to see them in the fullness of their inherent worth and dignity as human beings. In religious terms, we strive to affirm their holiness.

The distinction is a very fine line. It's subtle. It's personal. We can only determine it for ourselves. We have to be honest with ourselves and ask, "What am I really doing in this relationship? Am I making someone else carry my stuff? Am I making someone my Sherpa, using them to pay a cost that really should be mine to pay? Am I appropriating them, carrying them off for some purpose that's not theirs but that's really all about me? Am I failing to see the face of God in them and, in this sense, stealing them and violating this commandment?" By asking these questions, not only about people we know but people to whom we are connected through the economy on the other side of the planet, we begin to combat the alienation of the modern world.

The dual nuance of the phrase *lo tignov* brings a spiritual depth to the political questions of minimum wage and fair trade. When we cheat somebody out of the pay that is their due, we not only steal *from* him, but in a sense, we steal *him*. We utilize him for our personal gain, objectify him, and instrumentalize him. He becomes merely a means.

Stealing from YHVH

As we've seen, rabbinic tradition teaches that the Ten Commandments were not intended only to be read vertically, one through ten, but also horizontally across the two stone tablets, five on each one. (See page 185.) Each commandment about our relationship with people has a corresponding commandment about our relationship with God. In this reading, "Do not steal" is side-by-side with "Do not take the name of YHVH, your God, in vain."

The connection between the two might not be immediately obvious. But recall that the verb *nasa* in the third commandment, which is translated as "take," actually means "pick up and carry off," as in a commercial transaction. The word *lashav*, translated "in vain," means outside of its proper meaning or without the holiness that should be there. So that commandment is about appropriating or stealing God's name in a way that nullifies the holiness that should be there. Do not use YHVH opportunistically for your own personal gain. These two commandments are flip sides of the same coin. We are taught to preserve both YHVH and humans as ends in themselves, holy and complete. We should not use either as mere means to an end, stealing them for our own purposes, making them carry our cultural baggage.

The natural world is a direct emanation of YHVH— the ecosystems, the kaleidoscopic biological diversity, the natural food chains, and the balanced interplay of elements are the face of Reality to us and the living, loving matrix in which we are cradled. The natural world is an end in itself. It does not exist only as a means to our ends. It is not a resource only to serve our pleasure. Each creature, each blade of grass, according to Jewish mystical tradition, has its own reason for being. In fact, the mystics say that each blade of grass is so important, so holy, such a unique and treasured manifestation of life that every single one has an angel continually hovering over it whispering, "Grow! Grow! Grow!" Each one has inherent worth. So too does each human, each birch tree, each polar bear, each sea turtle, as well as the earth's ecosystems as a whole.

With this understanding of the inherent value of the natural world, we are invited to accept what the earth gives us as gifts—the spectacular abundance of fruits and vegetables, grains and legumes, fire, and freshwater for drinking. But we are not to steal from the earth. We are not to take more than what is freely given. We are not to pick things up and carry them off for our own personal gain without "paying" for them by replenishing the life cycle. This means we practice sustainable agriculture without the toxic chemicals that force the land to give us more than it can. We eat mostly plants, lifting the devastating ecological burden and cruelty of industrial animal agriculture. We use significantly less energy—which entails reducing production and consumption—and transition to renewable energy sources (with compassionate accountability to fossil fuel workers). We end the practice of ripping open and extracting from the earth through mining, oil drilling, and fracking, all of which are violent forms of theft resulting in cascading planetary impoverishment.

Through this interpretation of the eighth commandment, to buy a rabbit-skin puffball is to steal, every bit as much as pilfering a cell phone. Even if one pays an exorbitant price for it, the purchased product required extraction of resources from the land, deployment of toxic dyes and resins, fossil fuel energy, and freshwater, as well as the exploitation of human workers and rabbits (all of whom had angels hovering over them, cheering them on). The "common goods" of healthy air and clean water were stolen from all of us, however minimally, in the name of the trivial privilege of hanging a fun fashion accessory from one's handbag. To purchase such a thing at any price is to steal from YHVH and from ourselves.

Because YHVH is Reality, Life, each one of us and each blade of grass, *every* theft is stealing from YHVH. No act of taking something that doesn't belong to us stays contained.

In the great coloring book of life, stealing, like violence and lying, doesn't color neatly inside the lines. The color bleeds and gets everywhere. Our thievery alienates us from others and our world over and over again. We remain in a dreamlike haze, never understanding our own position on the planet and our own role in the lives of others. We may not directly feel the effects in our lifetime. We may not be conscious of how our own lives are diminished. But our children and grandchildren will know that they live in a diminished world. We never ultimately "get away with it," because each of us is part of the whole from which we have stolen.

Paying for Our Stuff

The Nepali Sherpa Chhewang Nima was struck by an avalanche on his nineteenth ascent of Mount Everest. Once the search was called off, his widow was informed

211

of his death. He had been working for a veteran climber and after the accident she immediately came back down the mountain to go to the widow's house. She says that the wailing could be heard from down the street. The climber was devastated by what had happened. After thinking about it and talking with Chhewang Nima's family, she decided to put herself in the role of breadwinner for that family. Every year, she decided, she would give them the amount of money that Nima would have made working as a Sherpa. She has kept this promise. And she doesn't just send a check to Nepal. She goes in person each year to visit the family, pay her respects, and deliver the money. She is trying to treat him and them as ends in themselves and not just as means.

The eighth commandment is a challenge to each of us because, although most of us are not going to hire a Sherpa or buy a rabbit-fur pom-pom, almost all of us in Western culture purchase items that other people labor hard to make or come at great price to our ecosystems but for which we pay relatively little. Much of what we buy probably falls into this category and the benefits we receive from such products are relatively trivial. This does not mean we are bad people. It just means we are deeply entrenched in our culture.

What can we do about it? How can we cultivate a new consciousness in which other people, animals, and natural elements are not "resources" but constituents? How can we faithfully pay for our stuff?

One could cynically think that the climber who is now financially supporting Nima's family is only using them as a means to assuage her guilt. But it's likely that she was truly changed by what happened and she is trying to make amends in a deep and authentic way. Maybe through this family, she is recognizing the holiness in everyone. What more can we ask of ourselves than to recognize our mistakes and learn and grow from them? Luckily, when we use someone to carry our stuff, they generally don't die or become maimed as a result. We can examine what we're doing and make amends. We can look again at them and see their holiness. We have time to return what was stolen. We can review our own lives, relationships, and transactions and find ways to make amends.

Reversing the Current

If stealing is taking from YHVH, taking from people and from the life systems of our world, what is its inverse? What is the positive framing of the eighth commandment? What *should* we do? And to the extent that we have stolen, how *can* we make amends? It's not spelled out in the terse language of the commandment, but the mirror image of stealing must have something to do with giving. Instead of trying to take as much as we can from the systems around us, keeping the eighth commandment means putting as much as we can into those systems. Solar panels on a building can serve as a metaphor—at times, the panels create so much energy, drawn freely from the sun, that they reverse the usual flow of the current and send electricity back into the grid. Neighbors then receive that energy as a blessing. This reverse flow is the eighth commandment in the shimmering fullness of its expression.

To reverse the current, we strive to take into account the whole person. Rather than take advantage of a worker's vulnerabilities (like his inability to find higher-paying work), we honor his strengths. We see him as an end in himself. If we are in the position of the employer, we pay a salary that will enable him to live with dignity—a living wage that includes health care, time off to care for family, and a little extra to put by for the future. And if we are in the position of the consumer, we insist that the employers at all links of the supply chains of the products we enjoy pay humanely and fairly. Our insistence is expressed through our purchases and through direct political advocacy.

We will not do it perfectly. We are all embedded in systems that make theft, small and large, virtually impossible to avoid. Because of the theft already built into our agriculture systems, low-income people often cannot pay the prices that reflect organic and fair-trade production. Because of the theft already built into our transportation systems, we may need to drive a car to get to work, participating in the stealing of oil from the earth. We cannot buy electronics today without participating in theft through poverty wages somewhere in the world. But in this commandment, as with all the commandments, the important thing is that we do everything that we *are* able to do. This doesn't mean only everything that is comfortable or easy. Every one of us can find ways to give to the interconnected webs of which we are a part. We are not called to be perfect; we are called to set the intention to transact honestly and lovingly with others, with the earth, and with YHVH.

With this intention, humans can begin to resume our rightful place in the ecosystems of our world—a place in which we give and take in flow and balance. Each of us can begin to chip away at the walls of our alienation from one another—the people in our communities and on the other side of the planet. We can begin to look for every opportunity and every way to put love back into the system, becoming our siblings' keepers. We can proactively support health and vibrancy and fairness in public policy and law. And we can look for ways to vote with our wallets for positive economic processes—so that when we do need something, we pay for it in a joyful act of giving for all that conspired to create it. We can pay for things, not only to get, but also to put goodness into the system. In this way, we actively contribute to the life force of YHVH and the liberation of all.

The eighth commandment teaches us to pay our own way, carry our own stuff. *Lo tignov.* If we can't schlep our own gear up the mountain, we should probably leave the top of the world to heaven.

ED SHAKER

▼

The Ninth Commandment

Do Not Testify against Your Neighbor as a Lying Witness

▲

Speak and Demand Truth in Every Sphere—Home, Corporations, Government

Do not testify against your neighbor as a lying witness.

We live in a culture in which lying is acceptable. Spouses and partners lie to each other in order to be kind and avoid admitting that yes, that outfit makes you look fat. Parents lie to their kids to dodge a difficult conversation or to cultivate a magical myth about Santa Claus or the Tooth Fairy. Politicians lie to the electorate in order to win elections. And when spouses, children, or voters find out about the lie (and it's almost always a *when*, not an *if*), they generally shrug. It doesn't matter. Our cultural consensus is that lying is not evil and truth telling is not inherently good. It all depends.

Even the biblical commandment to not bear false witness against one's neighbor doesn't, in a literal reading, outlaw lying generally, but specifically when lying incriminates an innocent person. Most of the major medieval Jewish commentators don't even unpack this commandment, because its meaning is thought to be obvious. It's intended to preserve a court system that's reliable and just. One commentator, Ibn Ezra, notes that the verb can be read as causative—"to cause to testify falsely"—so it prohibits hiring a false witness as well as directly lying oneself. But it doesn't extrapolate to lying in general.

The fact that the commandment specifies "your neighbor" makes it seem narrower still. The commandment to not kill simply says, "Don't kill." It doesn't say, "Don't kill your neighbor." The commandment to not steal simply says, "Don't steal." It doesn't say, "Don't steal from your neighbor." These are absolute wrongs, regardless of whether the victim is your neighbor or not. But the ninth commandment says, "Do not testify against your neighbor as a lying witness (*ed shaker*)," which suggests that this is specifically about relationships within a community. The message seems to be that lying is not an absolute wrong like killing and stealing, but it is wrong within a community, perhaps because it damages relationships. Honesty is part of the glue that holds the fabric of a community together.

Against Your Neighbor

But on a deeper level, this commandment challenges us to do more than simply refrain from testifying falsely against someone we know in court, something few of us will ever have occasion to do. The language raises the timeless question of who, in spiritual terms, our "neighbor" is. Perhaps in biblical times, the neighbor was thought to mean only a member of one's immediate community or tribe. But the Hebrew word *rea* is sometimes used to refer broadly to a fellow human being or the "other." It can mean a companion here on earth. In Richard Elliott Friedman's Torah commentary, he points out that the Leviticus command to "love your neighbor as yourself" comes in close proximity with the command to love the stranger and the foreigner as oneself, as well. The ninth commandment is not just about the lies that we tell about and to people in our own communities. It means everyone.

In our globalized world, nothing stays confined to just one community. A tweet can turn an election. A law passed in the US can mean life or death in rural India. We are all neighbors. Our words of truth and falsehood, even when spoken to or about someone locally, can affect everyone everywhere.

There are many ways that a lie can serve as a weapon "against" one's neighbor. To tell lies against your neighbor is to say something untrue that will hurt someone else. Lying is rarely a victimless crime. Some person and some relationship are always at the other end of a lie. A lie that is completely without consequence either to the teller or the hearer would never be told to begin with.

When we bother to lie, it's because the truth is too difficult, uncomfortable, or momentous to utter; we are trying to get away with or cover up some nefarious act; or we are trying to protect ourselves. Something is always at stake when we lie, even when we think we are just lying to be kind. Unearth what that "something" is, and it usually has profound meaning for the liar, the lied to, or both.

Big Public Lies

In today's political climate there has been great slippage in the categories of truth and falsehood. Now there is a third, widely accepted category with its own term coined by comedian Stephen Colbert, now bearing the imprimatur of the Oxford English Dictionary: "truthiness." Truthiness is "the quality of seeming or being felt to be true, even if not necessarily true." A concept bearing truthiness gets wide latitude and respect in our culture. It is increasingly difficult to object to such a claim as a lie.

The kind of lying that inspired Colbert's invention of "truthiness" is public lying, usually on a grand scale. When a public figure falsely claims, for example, that a nation is harboring "weapons of mass destruction" or claims that a neighboring country is sending across the

221

border to the US primarily "drug addicts and rapists," he is in direct violation of the ninth commandment. He is acting as a lying witness against his neighbor. The neighbor, in both of these cases, is significantly harmed: in the first case, the Iraqi people suffered an invasion by the US with devastating consequences even today; in the second case, Latinos have become victims of increasing prejudice, discrimination, and even violence at the hand of other Americans.

And yet, at the time that they were uttered, each of these false claims had the vague ring of truthiness. The September 11 terrorists had indeed come from somewhere in the Arab world and so, Americans figured, someone over there deserved to be attacked. As we find in people of all nationalities, some Mexicans are rapists and some are addicted to drugs. So a couple of incriminating anecdotes combined with a general distrust of immigrants by some sectors of the US population made that claim truthy as well. The author of each of these lies was subsequently elected or reelected president of the United States. Their lies were identified as lies by large media outlets but millions of Americans shrugged and moved on.

People routinely excuse the steady stream of lies that we find in everything from fake news to fake scientific disagreements to corporate public relations campaigns that construct brazen inversions of a company's actual intentions. It's the nature of business; it's the nature of politics; it's the nature of the internet; it's human nature, we say. When we do this—when we endorse those who lie—we shift our own role in the story. We were the party lied to; now we become complicit in the lie itself. Worse, we become complicit in a culture that dilutes the very notion of truth and relativizes every fact. It's a cynical culture in which a person is expected to say whatever advances her individual agenda regardless of its basis in reality. It's a culture that renders the ninth commandment optional because the underlying concept of a clear delineation between truth and falsehood becomes unintelligible.

Undermining the Dominant Narrative

This slippage of truth has an ironic history. Postmodernism, the iconoclastic intellectual and artistic movement of the 1970s, cut its teeth deconstructing the conservative powers of white male Western European authority. It shredded triumphalist narratives about "mankind" and "progress" and the greatness of the United States. It elevated third-world voices, queer voices, and the voices of people of color. It eschewed high art in favor of populist art, professional culture in favor of youth culture, mainstream media in favor of alternative media. "The

Revolution Will Not Be Televised," according to an old bumper sticker. The old Enlightenment ideals of objective reality and truth were called into question as one supposedly objective fact after another was exposed as a mere fabrication serving the dominant powers' monopolies.

Cultural and moral relativism was a breath of fresh air and a taste of power for peoples who had found themselves always on the losing end of the established hierarchies of morality, beauty, and truth. But today, this revolution has been turned on its head. Far right conservatives, misogynists, and white supremacists have exploited the breakdown of authoritative sources of truth to advance their agendas. They have used social media, internet trolling, conservative media outlets like Fox News, and conservative talk radio shows like Rush Limbaugh's and Sean Hannity's to spread disinformation and sow seeds of doubt about factual knowledge.

It has become a vocation for some to create destabilizing online memes, consciously using the principles of postmodern theorists like Michel Foucault and Jacques Lacan to construct an alternative to the "dominant narrative." They have appropriated the rage of the postmodern movement, railing against what they call the "elite" and positioning themselves as the oppressed underclass (despite—and sometimes because of—the fact that they tend to be white and male). This campaign has effectively undermined the authority of public institutions and individuals who speak truth on behalf of those who are actually oppressed.

Exxon Knew

A treacherous instance of public dishonesty in our era—the quintessence of acting as an *ed shaker* against one's neighbor on a grand, operatic scale—is Exxon's decades-long endeavor to hide the science about climate change from the public. According to Harvard researchers Naomi Oreskes and Geoffrey Supran in the peer-reviewed journal *Environmental Research Letters*, as far back as the 1970s Exxon executives knew about the devastating global impact of the burning of fossil fuels. They knew that the full discharge of their corporation's business model would likely result in dramatic sea level rise, droughts, severe storms, and untold environmental damage.

Exxon's in-house climate expert warned in an internal memo that, should the public truly grasp the danger of climate change, stringent regulations would surely follow, which would be ruinous for the fossil fuel industry. The negative impact from those regulations on business will come sooner than from climate change itself. So they suppressed the scientific reports, hired scientists to conjure contradictory evidence, and, like the tobacco industry concealing the dangers of smoking, manufactured doubt in the public discourse despite the overwhelming evidence.

At the time that the Bible was written, one could not have imagined that testifying as a lying witness against one's neighbor could take on such outlandish proportions. (It's a curious twist that in this case, instead of falsely claiming guilt, the liar is falsely claiming innocence. But it amounts to the same thing.) It used to be that a lie in court risked the life of an innocent person wrongly accused. Today, a lie can risk the lives of millions of people with the misfortune of living in coastal communities or drought-prone plains. It can destroy entire ecosystems, drive animal and plant species to extinction, ravage farming communities around the world, and eventually lead to mass starvation. Such is the exponentially amplified power of words in our hyperconnected day. Insofar as the Ten Commandments were written as a public manifesto to ensure a healthy and just society, there is no more appropriate time to observe them than right now.

Nice, Private Lies

In our cultural taxonomy of lies, most of us would agree that lying to be able to keep doing something that could bring about the end of the world as we know it would be the worst kind of lie. Many would also agree that the least bad kind would be the lie that supposedly hurts no one and can even serve as a compassionate alternative to the truth. The "no, you look great in that dress, honey," is one version of this and the "yes, of course I remembered to come in and kiss you good night when I got home after you went to sleep" is another. These kinds of lies seem harmless because they are actually intended to help the person being deceived feel loved. These lies are private; they don't seem to affect anything beyond the person being lied to. Yet there is a direct connection between big public lies and the nice private lies. How could this be? The nice lie seems so innocuous. What could it cost anyone?

What it costs is our collective purchase on truth. It compromises the quality and authenticity of our relationships. It blurs the clarity of our understanding of one another and the world. It shakes our trust in YHVH—life itself—because we can't know what's real and what's not. Lies of any magnitude cloud the difference between reality and fiction, and promote the acceptance of truthiness.

In that proverbial case of the wife asking her husband if she looks fat in this dress—a scene that applies without regard to gender—the truth is that he thinks she does. Either she's asking an honest question and she really wants to know his opinion to help decide whether to wear the dress, or the question is code for a different question like, "Do you love me?" or, "Are you attracted to me?"

If she truly wants his opinion, he owes her his truth. She's explicitly asked for help in making a decision, she values his input, and if he cares about her, he shouldn't mislead her.

If what she's really asking is, "Do you love me?" or, "Are you attracted to me?" the issue is more complicated because she is not being honest with her question. She is not asking what she wants to know. So what to do? He could answer in code the question that she asked in code: play along with the game and answer, "No, you don't look fat," meaning, "Yes, I love you just the way you are." But in taking this admittedly easier approach and using social niceties as their private mode of communication, the husband inadvertently creates distance between them. The intimacy of the marriage is subtly diluted.

They both know on some level that she was not completely honest with him and that he was not completely honest back. A filter now sits between them that makes it harder for them both to see the other clearly or see a clear reflection of themselves in the other's eyes. The husband thinks he is lying "for" his wife by telling her what she wants to hear, but the lie does not serve her deeper interests. In this most intimate space of marriage, lies get in the way of truly knowing and being truly known, and the result can be profoundly lonely. When deep trust is unavailable in that most intimate relationship, the world—YHVH—can feel less trustworthy. The husband has been an *ed shaker* "against" his wife in that he has injected a rivulet of confusion and mistrust into her universe. A bolder and more spiritually grounded approach might be for the husband to say, "Yes, that dress is not flattering on you, and I love you very much no matter what you wear."

Perhaps she's speaking in code, and in fact the husband does *not* love her. Then it's even *more* essential that he be truthful. That would be the hardest truth to speak and to hear, but the most important. She has a right to know that truth. While a conversation about a dress might not be the best time to bring up existential threats to the relationship, the husband does his wife and himself a great disservice if he uses small lies to tell much larger, substantive lies. He might say, "I think you know my answer. Yes, that dress is not flattering on you," and find another time soon to talk honestly about their marriage.

We all have a right to know the truth. Even if we don't always want to hear the truth, those who speak to us are to speak truthfully to us. Well-intentioned lies deprive others of information they need to make good decisions. Every time we ask dishonest questions, inviting others to lie to us, we also lie "against" somebody—ourselves.

Lying to a Child

When a parent lies to a child, it's another version of the "nice, private" violation of the commandment. Imagine that a mother has promised to kiss her son good night when she comes home from work after he's already asleep. She forgets to do it. The boy asks her the next morning whether she did it. His real question, like that of the woman with the dress, is probably, "Do you love me?" (the indirect way of asking is not dishonesty in the case of a child). The mother replies, "Of course. I wouldn't forget." She wants him to feel loved. She fears his recrimination or disappointment. Perhaps she wants to pretend, even to herself, that she is the perfect parent who never forgets anything.

But in so doing, she deprives herself and her son of a precious moment of authentic connection and misleads him as to the nature of love. He is left believing that the fact that she remembered proves that she loves him. He is left believing that his mother always perfectly executes her plans. He is deprived of the lesson, so crucial for maturation, that even when we love someone, occasionally we fail them. The mother thinks she is lying "for" her son, when in fact she is inadvertently acting as an *ed shaker* "against" him.

Imagine if she had told him the truth instead: "No,

sweetie, actually I forgot. I'm sorry. I didn't forget about *you*, though—I thought about you many times last night." The boy would learn that his mother tells him the truth even when he doesn't want to hear it and—crucially—even when it would be easy to lie. He can trust her. Maybe he too can have the courage to tell the truth even when someone doesn't want to hear it. He would learn that his mother accepts her own imperfections. Maybe it's okay for him to be imperfect too. He would learn that love cannot be proven or disproven by a single symbolic gesture. He would learn that his relationship with his mother is not fragile. A good relationship can withstand the truth and even be strengthened by it.

What if, on the other hand, the mother's failure to remember that kiss is part of a larger pattern of failure to fulfill responsibilities to the child? What if, for example, she is an alcoholic and often drinking when she should be caring for him? The parent would then be using the smaller lie to tell a bigger lie: "Yes, I kissed you," meaning, "Yes, I am showing up for you in general as I should. There is no problem here." She would be gaslighting the child, making him second-guess his correct intuitions, giving him misinformation about the relationship with his parent. In this case, an honest conversation about the good-night kiss would be essential. It could expand to an honest conversation about the relationship and the parent's failings as a whole. This situation, in which telling the truth would be hardest, is the one where the truth would be most vital.

The Ascetic Practice of Truth Telling

The emotional challenge and spiritual intensity of truth telling have not been lost on religions over the ages. In many religious traditions, refraining from lying is considered an ascetic spiritual practice. We think of asceticism as fasting, extreme austerity, forgoing comforts, stripping down to the bare essentials of life. To recognize truthfulness as a form of asceticism and lying as a "comfort" is a powerful tool in spiritual growth.

To have the option of lying available at our fingertips *is* a comfort. Our social games and codes make life easier and smoother, in the short run. Socially acceptable lying allows us to imagine and pretend that we and others are better, smarter, kinder, closer, more thoughtful than we really are. We can exaggerate our successes and erase our failures, dodge responsibility for something that didn't go well at work or home, avoid facing the ways in which we misprioritize the different demands in our life.

In telling the truth, we are forced to be direct, to own what we want and think. We have to admit where we have fallen short and claim credit only where we have succeeded. We are challenged to confront the deeper issues in our relationships without hiding behind pleasantries. To address such deeper issues between spouses, parents, children, business colleagues, friends, or even enemies cultivates authentic relationships—the kinds of relationships we can depend on in hard times and be proud of at the end of our lives. We can know with certainty that when we are loved, that love is not based on a fiction, but grounded in the reality of who we are with all our imperfections.

Most of all, in telling the truth to others, we are forced to tell ourselves the truth. We examine our own motivations. When, for example, we admit to ourselves and then honestly tell our friend that we simply didn't make time to return his phone call when he was in need, it requires us to examine our values and how we spend our time. We have to consider how important that friendship is and how important friendship is, in general, in our lives. When we admit to our boss that we fudged our sales numbers, it requires us to take a hard look at our self-esteem, spiritual health, and even aptitude for the work we had felt compelled to fake.

The ascetic practice of truthfulness constantly reminds us and others that life is serious and short and we don't have time to say what we do not mean. It affirms our responsibility to ourselves to live honestly, not conjure a life we wish we had or invent a persona we wish we were. It acknowledges and honors our sacred connection to one another.

Lying does soul damage to the liar, the one lied to, and the relationship between them. By refusing to lie, we refuse to participate in such soul damage. Truthfulness teaches us that the sky doesn't fall when we reveal our shortcomings or tell others something hard to hear. It gives us the opportunity to learn from our mistakes, try to do better next time, and discover that our true self, honestly offered to the world, is more than good enough. The truth may cause big changes.

Exposing and Fixing Diseased Systems

The status quo is sustained when we forgive and even expect dishonesty. We permit diseased systems and relationships to stay in place by weaving lies to mask the symptoms. Majority-white institutions, for example, will claim that racial prejudice plays no role in hiring decisions. Managers give case-by-case rationales for how in each open position, the white candidate was "the right fit." Statistics, along with the experiences of people of color, controvert this claim. But even such self-deluding lies are usually accepted by the general public and help keep the system intact. The expectation that we will lie or cover wrongs with lies pervades our society from the most private corners to the most public stages.

If we were to take seriously the spirit of the ninth commandment and change this practice, we would all start to feel the symptoms. Painfully, embarrassingly, annoyingly, every social, psychological, and spiritual sickness of our culture would become apparent. If we all started telling the truth, as we saw it, about ourselves and others, the society we know would come unraveled and break down. But in most cases they would be the things that *should* unravel. What would survive would be those things that are true, enduring, and should survive.

Keeping this commandment is a spiritually audacious approach to life. It requires courage to let go of everything that isn't grounded in reality. It necessitates faith that it is going to turn out okay. "If you love something, set it free. If it comes back to you, it's yours. If it doesn't, it was never meant to be." It means cultivating compassion for ourselves so we admit to our own failings and weaknesses without undermining our inherent worth as human beings.

Some might say that ascetic truthfulness will only work if the entire culture or even the entire world agrees to practice it, and everyone at the same time. "Okay, everyone, count to three and then simultaneously start telling the truth about your work experience on your resumes and your age on dating websites." A lone truth teller in a lying world will get her lunch eaten. Like the speed of an athlete racing clean when everyone else is doping, the unenhanced performance may pale in comparison to the enhanced norm. This would be the fear, at least, and it could be justified. Sometimes telling the truth is punished in our society. Real losses are sometimes involved when one individual does the right thing and others do not. The ethical business leader is not always the most successful. Sometimes the sleazy, dishonest one dies with the most toys. Sometimes liars win.

This is why faith is essential. Faith teaches us that keeping a commandment, even when doing so entails sacrifice and pain, shapes a life worth living. We might "miss out" on things sometimes, yet the result will be a spiritually powerful, rich life. And the world around us will be transformed for the better. When the husband tells his wife the truth, it may signal a need for serious marital repair therapy. Even if they end up getting divorced, they may do so years earlier than if lies had masked their deepest conflicts; and each gets an earlier start to build a life in which they can be true to themselves. When the mother tells her son the truth about forgetting the good-night kiss, it could trigger a painful, much needed conversation that leads her to reckon with her alcoholism and transform her life and parenting. When the fossil fuel executive tells the truth about climate change, he loses his job but sets off a national outpouring of rage resulting in a just transition to a renewable-energy economy.

Ascetic truthfulness is not easy. Otherwise, we wouldn't need to be "commanded." The countercultural power of this commandment lies precisely in its difficulty. To refuse to act as an *ed shaker* requires us to rupture relationships grounded in falsehoods and eschew niceties when they entail deception. We are called to fix things that, for all anyone has said, ain't broke, and to withdraw our support, our money, and our votes from entities that lie, lest we become complicit in the lie. By keeping this ninth commandment and going against the accepted social norms of our society, we begin to create new norms. We reject the blur of truthiness. We reclaim the notion of truth as legitimate, holding ourselves and others accountable for what we and they say and do. Through the practice of ascetic truthfulness in all dimensions of our lives, we allow the natural energy of God to flow unobstructed through us and thereby shape reality.

LO TACHMOD

▼

The Tenth Commandment

Do Not Covet

▲

*Practice Your Liberation—
You Have Enough,
You Are Enough*

Do not covet your neighbor's house; do not covet your neighbor's wife, nor man-servant, maid-servant, ox, ass, or anything that is your neighbor's.

If you want to catch a monkey, there's an old tried-and-true technique developed in India. You take a coconut, cut a hole in it, and empty it out. You make the hole big enough for a monkey to fit his hand through when it's flat, but not when he makes a fist. You put a banana inside the coconut and attach the coconut to a tree. Then you hide and wait. When the monkey comes along, he will want that banana. He will reach in for it and find that once he's holding on to the banana, he's stuck. All he has to do is let go of the banana and he will be free. But apparently most monkeys can't let go. The tenth and final commandment is about letting go of the banana.

"Do not covet" (in Hebrew, *lo tachmod*) is the only commandment of the big ten that deals solely with an internal state. The first commandment probably comes closest in teaching that there should be no other gods "for us" or "to us" besides YHVH. But all the others, while they have significant spiritual dimensions, also deal directly with actions and behavior, what we should do and not do in order to lead meaningful lives and participate in the transformation of our world. *Lo tachmod* seems to pertain exclusively to what's going on in our own most secret, most private depths. It deals with desire. It addresses parts of ourselves that we may not be proud of, that we keep hidden. If we break this commandment, no one will know but us; and seemingly no one but us will be affected.

Some of us might object on principle to the idea that our feelings should be legislated and argue we can only control what we do—and sometimes not even that—not how we feel. Efforts to change our feelings, some say, risk becoming repressive and are bound to fail.

This idea that we are overcome like rag dolls by our emotions and desires has its origins perhaps in nineteenth-century Romanticism. Today it's an idea trafficked by ad agencies, teenage poets, and strands of psychology that emphasize the virtues of acknowledging and honoring our feelings but warn against efforts to change them.

The assumption underlying *lo tachmod* is that we actually do have such agency in our internal life just as we do in our actions. Spiritual teachers from many traditions over the ages have taught that through spiritual practice, we can change how we feel and change our internal state. The ancient Israelites must have believed that humans have a free will so profound that it reaches inward even to the bedrock of our being.

Legislating Feelings

Rabbis over the centuries have wrestled with the notion that our internal state or feelings should be the direct object of a commandment. It seems out of character for Jewish law. Judaism is a religion of practices; it matters what we *do*, not how we feel about it. Interpreting the tenth commandment, some medieval rabbis were so uncomfortable they devised work-arounds. Some explained that to violate this commandment requires, not just a thought or feeling, but some actual act. If we covet our neighbor's record collection and pressure them into selling it to us, even if we pay for it, *that's* a violation of this commandment. Our coveting caused them to give up their precious LPs, which they did not really want to do. If we covet our neighbor's record collection and then we go ahead and steal it, the coveting is tacked on to the violation of the stealing itself, making the stealing a more grievous offense, as driving drunk exacerbates a moving violation.

Other rabbis have explained the tenth commandment as a kind of gatekeeper that protects us from doing things that are actually wrong. It's a buffer zone around the other commandments, called a *gezeirah*. If you don't even covet your neighbor's iPad, you're definitely not going to steal it. If you don't even covet your sister's husband, you're definitely not going to sleep with him. It is common in Jewish law to prohibit a smaller offense in order to prevent a bigger offense. Picking up a writing implement, for example, is prohibited on Shabbat in some circles, not because it's inherently problematic to pick up a pen, but because if we don't pick up a pen, we can be absolutely sure that we won't start writing and then inadvertently slip into some form of work.

This approach only works—like setting a clock ten minutes ahead to try to get to work on time—if we actually believe the ruse. We convince ourselves that the goal of not coveting is an end in itself, and then do everything in our power to address the problem.

Don't Think about a White Rabbit

Coveting is not just *any* feeling of wanting something. For a hungry person to want a meal or a homeless person to want a place to live is not coveting. Despite the fact that *tachmod* is sometimes translated as "desire," it is also not desire of just any kind. To desire to have sex with one's partner or to eat a strawberry from a wild strawberry plant is not coveting. Coveting is desire for things we should not have, which are not ours, to which we are not entitled, or which would harm someone else or the earth. Coveting is desire for things and people prohibited by other commandments. Coveting is any desire that keeps us trapped, like the monkey desperately gripping the banana.

We all covet. We all crave things that we don't have, shouldn't have, don't need, and sometimes that belong to someone else. We can covet someone else's success at work or their appearance or their seemingly problem-free children. Or we can covet someone else's entire life as they represent it at a party or on Facebook.

The paradox of this commandment is that even thinking about what we shouldn't covet awakens coveting within us. It's like being told, "Don't think about a white rabbit" and then we can think of nothing else. Thinking about not thinking about something makes you think about it. And the biblical commandment spells out exactly what you're supposed to not covet. You're supposed to not covet your neighbor's house, wife (presumably husband as well), ox, donkey, servant, or anything that belongs to your neighbor. What better way to make someone covet something than to

say, "See that? You can't have it and you can't want it."
It almost feels unfair. We can't will ourselves to keep
this commandment. Simply deciding to not want something won't work. We cannot keep this commandment
directly in the same way that we can directly not steal
or not lie.

We need to take an oblique approach—to create conditions in our lives that will support an inner shift. As
with all of the commandments, this entails a transformation that is both spiritual and political. We need to
avail ourselves of all the spiritual tools out there to cultivate our sense of "enoughness." And we need to become
wise to the social forces working against us, encourag-
ing our sense that we don't have enough and we aren't
enough, stimulating a bottomless desire for more.

We could extrapolate from this commandment
a piece of self-help advice: "Do not covet your neighbor's stuff, because coveting like this will make you
and others miserable. Longing for things that you can't
and shouldn't have will keep you in a perpetual state of
restless desire that will render you unable to appreciate
the gifts you do have in your own life." It is fitting that
at the end of the list of the important practices for our
relationship with God and with others, we are taught to
attend to ourselves spiritually and communally. To live
the good life, we need to use all the tools we have at our

disposal to find gratitude for what we have and not live in constant craving for something else.

Such tools include morning prayer, simply thanking God for returning our soul to us for another day on earth, and, in Jewish tradition, prayer in the afternoon and evening as well. Sabbath, too, is a practice that allows us to enter the beauty of what is, instead of grasping after something else. Gratitude. Awe. These sensibilities counter the covetousness within us. But they only carry us so far.

Coveting and Consumerism

Coveting is to corporate capitalism what sexism is to patriarchy—the very spiritual and psychological substance that fuels its existence. Coveting is the lifeblood of our economic and social structures. To keep the corporate engines humming, consumers must consume constantly and increasingly. We have to do exactly what, in fact, we do in the United States: spend over one trillion dollars per year on nonessential goods, accumulate hundreds of thousands of items in each private home, throw away over fifty pounds of clothing per year each, give our kids almost half of the world's toys even though they make up only a tiny fraction of the world's child population, and produce hundreds of millions of tons of waste each year. We need to also be willing, as we apparently are, to pay billions for services that help us attain the self-image and lifestyles we covet—dry cleaning, pizza delivery, weight-loss programs, streaming movies and music, fitness classes, and self-improvement apps. If we all suddenly failed to do this for one year, our economy as it is currently configured would collapse.

To consume at this ferocious rate, our decision to buy cannot be rational. It can't be based on our actual needs nor can it unduly factor in other considerations, such as the ecological or social impacts of what we're buying. Our consumption cannot weigh whether the purchase will actually make our lives better or consider the effects on our own freedom. To buy a product must feel vital, personal, and absolutely necessary. The experience must be rewarding, even chemically rewarding through the release of dopamine. We must suffer social consequences for not buying it and feel somehow lacking, as if everyone else has it. We have to feel that in a small way the purchase brings us closer to some ideal to which we aspire. By consuming, we will become who we want to be. This is what it means to covet today.

This complex and powerful emotion does not just happen by itself. It has to be systematically generated by the economic system that depends on it for survival. The ongoing stimulation of desire is built into the systems that create the objects of desire. This happens not only through deliberate marketing and advertising by particular companies for particular products, but through mass media, social media, and the aggregate power of our peers displaying their consumer lives in public. These together represent for us what success, happiness, and normal look like and they conspire to create a world where what we crave and own become the medium of our existence. The journey between craving and owning, and the resulting tension, is the great drama of our being.

Bringing a Knife to a Gunfight

Our consumer cravings for the most part are not natural like a monkey's for a banana; they are manufactured. An actual monkey's desire for a banana is more akin to our desire for sex, nurturing human touch, safety, or calories. These are physical and psychological needs that long predate the invention of commodities. As cravings, they can certainly take dangerous forms, but they are intrinsically life sustaining and necessary. They are not the "coveting" cautioned against by the tenth commandment. The coveting targeted in this commandment is unnatural. It causes our lives to fall out of balance as we pursue empty priorities, always striving for the next thing. Our cup is never full. By trying to acquire the things we covet, we become part of the normalizing, materialistic engine of our culture. We become part of the system that reifies the power of commodities, driving coveting in others.

Self-help philosophies and pop psychology overlook this when they define both the problem and solution as personal. To cast coveting as an individual vice is to miss its systemic nature. We do not simply crave people or things in a vacuum, personally, because of a lack of spiritual evolution or emotional maturity. Our craving exists in a social context, both intentionally and unintentionally induced by the entirety of the culture in which we live. The pressure on every one of us is immense.

It begins when we are small children who absorb, seemingly through the ether, messages about our inadequacies and the glittery, salvific properties of commodities. Pokémon cards bring status on the playground, some cards are more powerful than others, and their power transfers directly to the cardholder. Comparison pressure continues through our teen years and adulthood, conveying that our bodies aren't thin enough, our clothes aren't flattering enough, our skin isn't clear enough, our jobs aren't prestigious enough, our accomplishments pale next to those of others.

Our entire consumer culture, which is now global, stimulates coveting and we are all simultaneously victims and purveyors of it. Spiritual practices, including meditation and prayer, that seek to cultivate gratitude and a sense of contentment were developed before mass media, focus groups, game theory, Facebook/Twitter/Instagram; before biochemists were intentionally concocting recipes for addictive foods and teams of PhD psychologists were designing brands to trigger our deepest, most primal longings. Ancient spiritual practices were not designed to handle the current magnitude of countervailing force. To rely on such practices to resist the juggernaut of commercial culture is to bring a knife to a gunfight.

Some elite practitioners of mystical traditions may certainly access transcendence through years of rigorous discipline and escape the cycle of coveting. As Rabbi Lawrence Kushner, a scholar of Kabbalah, puts it, "You don't have an experience that is unitive in which you feel yourself dissolved into the divine all, and emerge from that wanting to rip somebody off." But ordinary spiritual practitioners who, outside of their practice time, participate fully in the media and social domains of our culture—going to work, buying groceries, watching TV, shopping online, browsing social media, going to the gym, doing school parties and sports activities with their kids—don't stand a chance. To keep the tenth commandment requires us to take our faith practices to another level entirely.

Building an Outside to the Culture of Coveting

For all the reasons discussed here, *lo tachmod* is an almost impossible challenge. We can't will ourselves to do it, and daily prayer, weekly yoga, adult coloring books, or nightly gratitude journaling won't offset the entire political and cultural might of corporate capitalism. To keep any of the commandments, and especially this one, we must take a more radical step. We need to lovingly shelter ourselves from the dominant culture.

Faith in our own internal childlike goodness—our own natural connection to God—will bloom once protected from the distortions of social conventions. We need to protect our families, as well, as much as we are able. The shield can be porous; we don't have to live in a shack in the Canadian Rockies and subsist on nuts and berries. Somewhere on the continuum between off-the-grid and full absorption in consumer society lies a sweet spot. Each of us must discover how we can both stay in our lives and find a modicum of freedom from material tyranny.

Almost every religious tradition has a precedent for disengagement from society. Religious communities have almost always started out countercultural, renouncing the idolatries of the secular world. In the early Christian community described in the book of Acts, people were so inspired by the teachings of Jesus that they completely broke from their social context:

> They were all filled with the Holy Spirit and spoke the word of God with boldness... No one claimed private ownership of any possessions, but everything they owned was held in common... There was not a needy person among them, for as many as owned lands or houses sold them and brought the proceeds of what was sold... It was distributed to each as any had need. (Acts 4:31–35 NRSV)

Being Christian was not initially seen as compatible with a normal life, having possessions, working an ordinary job, or even owning land. It was to have an entirely different vision of what it means to live.

Similar visions have animated the kibbutz movement in Israel and ashrams in India. Monastic traditions have reappeared repeatedly in different forms, through different religions throughout history. But sadly, the trajectory of these movements is almost always one of decline—the commitment fades, the momentum fizzles, the teachings ossify. Over time, people find it too hard to stand so alienated from the lives they once knew. The sacrifices are too great. Religion loses its radical edge as its institutions become ensconced in mainstream society. Liberal religion in our era has slid down that familiar slide, becoming liberal about liberalism.

Progressives' Embrace of Secular Culture

Religious liberals and political progressives tend to feel discomfort rejecting secular culture, because faith-based rejections have historically sported a socially conservative agenda. Conservative religious communities intentionally keep a distance from mainstream society often as a prophylactic against old-school social "evils"—sexual expressions, for example, that progressives would proudly celebrate. Individuals who breach the religious orthodoxy can wind up dangerously isolated. Mainstream, conservative religion has seemed to progressives like a throwback to more repressive times.

Religious liberalism has happily allied itself with secular culture because of a common emphasis on the rights of the individual and shared values concerning progressive social mores—LGBTQ rights, reproductive rights, premarital sex, divorce, antiracism, immigration protections, antiwar and antipoverty initiatives, and occasionally environmental protections. The secular world has represented progress.

But here the wires get crossed. Secular culture gives lip service to protecting all of these values but its economic and social systems exploit. Conversely, while some religious communities practice their traditions in ways that reinforce oppressive structures, some also build genuinely loving, place-based, multigenerational communities that resist consumerism and prize conservation.

When we redeploy the truly progressive powers of texts like the Ten Commandments in religious community, religion can offer both spiritual freedom and political muscle. The radical, life-sustaining, earth-honoring, liberating powers of religion can again be uniquely revolutionary in our era. But first we need the courage and the will to clear a space for it to thrive.

Creating Religious Countercultural Space

To create religious countercultural space requires, first and foremost, that we distance ourselves from the culture of coveting. Modern people can do this in many ways—there is no inherently right or wrong way. But one rule of thumb: if it feels easy to do, we're not going far enough. The work of carving out free space for ourselves and our families is hard work. It entails resistance to powerful forces that have guided our lives since infancy. We will know we are on the right track if the practices we undertake feel challenging but doable and we find ourselves, bit by bit, feeling a little freer and craving our old ways less and less. We may eventually find ourselves becoming so spiritually strong and so internally free that we can "reverse the current," sending our transformative, loving power out into the world.

The following are examples of practices for creating such space for ourselves:

- Recognize all entertainment as cultural "edutainment," educating us as to who we are, who we should be, and what we should covet. Tightly titrate the onslaught of media images and information. Get rid of television, especially in households with children. Limit music and movies to those that critique cultural norms and skip those that traffic in, celebrate, and reinforce cultural norms.
- Limit our news intake to basic information and critical analysis, opting out of the titillating dramas and vapid sensationalism.

- Use social media and browse the internet with restraint, knowing that the culture of coveting also permeates these spaces.
- Set a nonnegotiable power-down time each evening, turning off all our screens and reclaiming nonvirtual space for ourselves.
- Keep a joyful, no-exceptions Sabbath each week, preferably with family and friends.
- Avoid browsing in malls or department stores with all of their sparkling, enticingly displayed products. Remember that teams of psychologists, marketing experts, and game theorists have spent decades designing these spaces to stimulate coveting.
- For the most part, stop buying things. Acquiring something that we covet never quells the coveting. It functions like a drug where we continually need more to get the same high. When we truly need an object, buy it used or hand-me-down so that the brand luster has worn off.
- Avoid computer games, again designed by experts to produce addiction, inducing us to crave and pursue little hits of dopamine.
- Avoid professional sports or any sports other than casual pickup games that entice us into

passionate and purposeless competition—the spiritually ruinous world of winners and losers.

- Avoid spaces with people whose presence stimulates coveting. This will be a different set of people for each of us, but generally it means people who project impossibly perfect lives and generate insecurity in others—people whose shiny outsides tempt us to compare our marbled insides.

- Avoid social environments that stimulate sexual desire for people with whom we can't or shouldn't be sexual. Cultivate erotic intensity with our partner or would-be partner.

Most of the aforementioned practices are different versions of a single principle: any time we have a choice between a mediated experience of life and a direct experience, we choose the direct experience. Go for an in-person conversation rather than an email; a run outdoors instead of the elliptical at the gym; a children's playdate climbing trees instead of in a playground; an evening walk rather than streaming a show; back-country skiing rather than downhill; the local shopkeeper rather than the chain; biking rather than driving. The underlying theological assumption here is that if we can simply carve out open space in our lives, YHVH will rush into that space. Our own natural innocence and inherent goodness will well up within us. We will become more joyful, more connected, freer from coveting, and a more powerful force in the world.

Many of these unmediated experiences, ironically, are less available to lower-income people—the mediated world is often the most inexpensive and readily accessible world. This is one of the great systemic injustices against the poor. In poor neighborhoods, for example, there may only be concrete playgrounds (if that) and no trees to be found. There may be only fast-food chains, bodega groceries, and no farmers' markets. But most people can choose to sit on their stoop or go for a walk instead of watching TV. And anytime we do have a choice, no matter how small the choice, leaning toward the direct connection with God and nature, away from socially constructed environments, will be fresh air for our souls and a breath of freedom from all that we covet.

Those of us who have the privilege of operating further outside of the dominant culture have an obligation to stay engaged in the wider society, if only to advocate for the children who only have access to treeless playgrounds, or no playgrounds at all. We will not have built a real, spiritual "outside" to society until everyone can get there. The idea is not just to disengage ourselves, but

to work toward a changed culture. The Ten Commandments do not call us to build a shack in the Canadian
Rockies; they call us to stick around and help build the
liberation for everyone.

Community Is Crucial

They say that if you eat healthily and exercise regularly
and don't drink or smoke, you can practically live forever...or maybe your life will be so miserable, it will
just feel like it. To some of us, the ideas suggested here
for practicing the tenth commandment and creating
an "outside" to the dominant culture may sound like a
recipe for just such a miserable life. Any possible spiritual benefit would be outweighed by that manifest mis-
ery. And in fact, it *would* be a life without many of the
pleasures to which people in affluent nations are accustomed. Movies, for example, that traffic in and reinforce
cultural norms tend to be the most fun. They also happen to be the majority of the movies out there. And life
without bacon, as a friend put it, is simply less glorious.
To try to live with one foot outside of our culture might
feel joyless, overly serious, or even punitive. It would be
prohibitively hard for many of us.

This is why, although the commandments are
addressed to each of us in the singular, they need to

be practiced collectively. No one can do it alone, no one should do it alone, and, most importantly, no one would want to. Part of the strategy has to be building communities of people who share the dream of spiritual and political liberation. Within these gatherings, where everyone is, for example, keeping a Sabbath together, a simpler, noncoveting life can be joyful. When it becomes the norm for friends to share a walk or play music together instead of going to a bar or a movie, the friendships become more meaningful. When children grow accustomed to playing outside together instead of staring at screens, they will be happier. We can create real community together, something that is very hard to come by in today's world.

Communities of people intentionally embodying a religious counterculture can inspire each other, cheer each other on, hold one another accountable, and practice forgiveness for ourselves and one another when we slip, as we will, over and over again. This is hard stuff— at times, even, impossible. We are creatures of our culture, we have human needs and drives, and few of us are spiritual superheroes. We will not be perfect, or even close. We are likely unable to keep even a single commandment in its full expression. The journey will be always asymptotic—perpetually traveling toward our destination but never making it all the way.

Raising Noncoveting Children

Parenting in affluent countries in this unprecedented age of abundance and leisure can be challenging. Many parents struggle to balance our desire to give our children all the material and educational advantages we can afford with our desire to raise children who are hardworking, principled, grateful for what they have, and compassionate toward others. Modern life does not give middle-class children natural lessons in delayed gratification, nor does it provide them opportunities for useful work that contributes to the family and community, nor does it help them understand the difference between "needs" and "wants." Quite the opposite: our society produces children who covet, who feel entitled to what they covet, and who often get what they covet.

And just as small lifestyle tweaks won't suffice for adults to begin to escape the culture of coveting, they won't work for kids either. Parents who want our children to grow up with a sense of internal dignity, in which they are not blown off their feet by every passing social zephyr, need to be prepared to confront some serious headwinds. These headwinds will come from our parental peers, from the children's peers, and from the children themselves. In a society in which almost every experience of YHVH is filtered through human institutions (from playgrounds to schools to movies to museums), allowing our kids unmediated experiences can be a powerful antidote.

Bring them to the woods or a beach or even an abandoned lot without any agenda; let them play in the dirt or build stuff out of rocks, old cans, and fallen branches. These things are rarely as dangerous as we think they are. Take walks with them in the city with no destination. Spend unstructured time with children. Give them jobs to do. Let them hang out with us while we do errands and chores, rather than enrolling them in programs and structured activities. These are sacred gifts for them. Just get civilization out of their way and let them grow.

Given the alternative of immersion in a spiritually impoverished culture, the tenth commandment calls us to shelter ourselves and our children, to carve out space for the possibility of a new consciousness to germinate. The notion of "sheltering" our children has a negative ring to it these days. But this sheltering is not the timid kind that some well-meaning parents attempt—sheltering children from knowledge of death or sex or from hard work or failures or physical dangers. These are the many faces of YHVH, and children should be encouraged to experience them (although physical danger, obviously, only to a point). We are called to shelter them, instead, from consumer culture and media that induce insecurity and craving. Disney is far more dangerous than running barefoot outside. *Teen Vogue* is more dangerous than eating a little dirt. McDonald's is more dangerous than talking to strangers.

Perhaps the most powerful way to raise our children in freedom from coveting is to model it ourselves. It is well-known that kids learn from example more than anything. In the midrash, the practice of example setting is cast as the rationale for the entire Ten Commandments: "Be no thief, nor the accomplice or companion of thieves, that your children may not become thieves." "Be not adulterers, nor the accomplices or companions of adulterers, that your children after you may not be adulterers." "Do not associate with murderers, and shun their companionship, that your children may not learn the craft of murder." Committing ourselves to compassion and liberation, and surrounding ourselves with a community of people who are similarly committed, *so that* we can pass those values on to our children is the whole point. Our children are our best hope for creating a new world.

Through the eyes of the next generation, whether biological children or other children in our lives, we have a possibility to encounter the world afresh. And we have a responsibility to help keep them safe from the true dangers that lie ahead—the social forces that threaten to harden them, disillusion them, fill them with an aching need for the approval of others, and stimulate coveting within them. If it's only for their sake that we reorient our lives around YHVH and try to expand our own consciousness, that's reason enough.

Perhaps we will, in the course of it, transform ourselves. Perhaps we will find that what we used to covet wasn't so great after all and that the people and things we already have in our lives are blessings beyond measure. Perhaps we can become dizzy with gratitude over the simplest of gifts—the ability to walk down the street and smell a faraway restaurant in the breeze, the taste of a snowball, the warmth of someone else's hand in our own. Perhaps over time we can feel like we finally have enough and reclaim a wisp of our own lost innocence.

CHESED

▼

Conclusion: Kindness to the Thousandth Generation

▲

It was a strange and historic moment one morning in 1995 when a long truck pulled into Yellowstone National Park carrying eight Canadian wolves. This shipment of wolves had been for years the focal point of explosive political battles and the stuff of dreams for wildlife biologists. After many false starts and almost-dashed hopes, the day had finally arrived. Nobody knew what exactly would happen. This had never been tried before. One of the biologists' fears was realized right away: when they released the pack, the alpha couple, a male and a female who was pregnant, immediately headed north and crossed out of the park, trying to head home. The male got shot by a rancher, illegally. But the rangers eventually found the female and the pups and returned them to the safety of the park. That couple and those pups are the ancestors of many of the wolves in Yellowstone today.

Wolves had been hunted to eradication in Yellowstone by 1930 and for almost seventy years there were no wolves in the park. During that time, the health of the ecosystem and many species had declined. Elk, free from their predators, had munched the trees and bushes around waterways down to stubs; the beavers no longer had good materials to make their dams and so were failing; the numbers of fish and animals that live in the water had dropped dramatically; birds of all kinds were struggling. The banks of the rivers had eroded and the rivers had become shallower and slower. Everything was slowing and declining. It was as if the life force in the entire region was fading.

Biologists had long known that wolves were the missing puzzle piece in the Yellowstone ecosystem. They had long studied the virtuous cycle created by top-level predators—a cascade of positive impacts that maintain an entire ecosystem in health and balance. But the idea of reintroduction faced significant resistance from ranchers and the public generally. The scientists had to fight hard to combat the fears. An environmental group offered to compensate ranchers for any wolves' depredations. Finally, they prevailed. The biologists who dreamed this up had the courage and the vision and the strength of their convictions to create the possibility for an extraordinary chain of events:

The pack of wolves that arrived that morning thrived and grew and eventually reached a robust population. As the wolves came back, one by one plants along the riversides, the beavers, and all the other animals, fish, and birds began to return as well. Even the elk fared well—they just hid more in the deeper forests and didn't linger snacking by water. The rivers themselves changed shape—they became deeper and faster flowing, with more estuaries that support wildlife and more sharply defined banks because of better soil that was eroding less. This small group of wolves, simply by being themselves and doing what wolves do, brought balance back to the ecosystem and life back to the earth. The biologists had tipped the first domino and nature took care of the rest.

What Does It Matter What I Do?

Some of us suspect that even if we *did* do our very best to center YHVH and the power of liberation in our lives, even if we *were* able to transcend our own coveting and trade fairly for the goods we consume, become ascetic truth tellers, keep our sexual commitments, and keep a Sabbath, and even if we *did* find it all personally "worth it" because of greater joy, freedom, dignity, and purpose in our lives, it wouldn't really do anything to change the wider world. Systemic injustice would still be in place, world hunger would persist, the earth's ecosystems would still be teetering on the edge of their ability to sustain life. We would have gone to great lengths, sacrificed much, and accomplished nothing in the big picture.

Here the biblical tradition disagrees. If there is any

thread that runs throughout the Torah text and the midrash and commentaries it is that individual humans matter—we matter and our actions matter in ways much broader and deeper than we could ever know. It matters what we say, it matters what we do, it matters what we eat, what we buy, and with whom we have sex. Every decision we make ripples out through a world that is dense with meaning. We shape the very fabric of reality, for better and for worse.

The second commandment—the one prohibiting the making of sculpted images—includes the following warning: "for I, YHVH, your God, am an impassioned God, visiting the guilt of the fathers upon the children, to the third generation and to the fourth generation of those who hate me." Many of us bristle at the idea of God as a "being" who judges and punishes, particularly one who would punish children for things their parents and grandparents did. But when we look at the world, that is indeed how things work. Remember that God here is YHVH—Reality. It is a tragic reality that children suffer because of their parents' actions. There is a transfer of pain across the generations. The rejection of God, or call it the inability or unwillingness to access compassion and love, is never confined to one act or one person: it always affects the world to the third or fourth degree of separation.

When a parent is abusive or absent or simply doesn't know how to love, that pain often transfers to the children and then the grandchildren and then the great-grandchildren. So many of us in this world are third- and fourth-generation inheritors of pain like that. In what Freud called the "repetition compulsion," we tend to treat others how we ourselves were treated. Even when the original wound is no fault of the ancestors, the pain can metastasize throughout a community for a century or more. African-American descendants of slaves are still suffering from the violence of that enslavement generations ago. And many of those in contact with those communities are still perpetuating the spiritual distortions of racism that gave rise to it. Violence and evil don't stay put in history or geography—they breed and multiply.

But what saves the day here, literally the saving good news of faith, is that goodness and love also multiply. Our religious traditions teach us that yes, hate proliferates, but that love proliferates exponentially more. The full biblical text that concludes the second commandment reads, "for I, YHVH, your God, am an impassioned God, visiting the guilt of the fathers upon the children, to the third generation and to the fourth generation of those who hate me, but showing loving-kindness to the *thousandth* generation of those who love me and those who keep my commandments."

Pain travels to the third or fourth generation, but loving-kindness (in Hebrew, *chesed*) travels to the *thousandth*. This too rings true in our world. When we act out of love, justice, truthfulness, and respect, that goodness reverberates outward into the galaxy, touching everyone and everything. And the corollary to this is that we are the beneficiaries of goodness from long, long ago. Many of us know people who are sane, loving people, good partners or good parents who, themselves, came from an abusive family. And we ask, "How did she turn out to be such a good partner?" "How did he turn out to be such a good father?" "Where did she get such self-confidence?" "Where did he get such strength?" The thousandth-generation principle teaches that it could have been a powerful love a hundred years ago that formed a substrate of compassion, kindness, strength, and pride that transmitted silently through the generations to that person. Goodness proliferates. *Chesed* can never be contained.

When I feel daunted by the difficulty of keeping the commandments, when I am skeptical that anything I could do could positively affect the giant systems of our world, I think of this sacred teaching and I think of the story of the wolves in Yellowstone, in which one small but bold act opened the floodgates to a torrent of goodness. Each of these narratives reminds me that YHVH has a stake in the outcome of life on earth. YHVH is not indifferent, but is constantly pushing toward wholeness, healing, and liberation from oppression. YHVH is the God who brought us out from a house of slaves. We are not on our own in our struggles: the work that we do, like a year-end donation to a nonprofit, will be more than matched by a very generous donor. As nature can do so much with so little, we too can do much with little when we are working in the flow of YHVH. When we perform even one small act of courageous love, it can trigger a cascade of goodness that pours into our lives and out to our families, to our communities, and to the ecosystems of the world itself... not just to the third or fourth, but to the thousandth generation.

Ten Blessings

Recall that in Jewish tradition, the Ten Commandments are known simply as ten *devarim*—words, things, or concepts for living a holy and meaningful life. To the extent that we have the capacity and the resources, they function as commandments, challenging us to change and grow. But to the extent that we are hurting or lost—to the extent that we need the nurture of YHVH, the perspective swivels. We can hear in the voice from Mount Sinai a loving consciousness gently stirring us, inviting us, calling us with *chesed* toward our own liberation. The commandments, like a sleeve inverting itself, transform into blessings:

May you be blessed with power directly from the tap—the Source of life and liberation; may it, and nothing else, guide you.

May you be blessed with authenticity; may you be able to discern the real from the simulation.

May you be blessed with innocence; may you always speak the goodness of life and break free from cynicism.

May you be blessed with peace; may you luxuriate in sacred time and space every week.

May you be blessed with humility; may you honor your Source in all its forms.

May you be blessed with compassion; may you be a life-sustaining force for all the creatures of the earth.

May you be blessed with love; may you repair what is broken and cherish what is imperfect.

May you be blessed with abundance; may you never need to take what is not yours.

May you be blessed with honesty; may you be a conduit for the voices of truth in your world.

May you be blessed with enough; may you always be filled with the freedom, joy, and dignity of YHVH.

Acknowledgments

I am grateful beyond measure to the people and powers who conspired to make this book a reality. I am grateful, first, to my editor, Adrienne Ingrum, whose enthusiasm has been a lifeline and whose edits made the manuscript sharper and smoother at the same time. To Ellen Geiger, my literary agent, who took a flyer on me and invested her wisdom and care into this project.

I thank the congregation at First Unitarian Congregational Society in Brooklyn for not only tolerating a sermon series on the Ten Commandments, but engaging it with open hearts. It was because of their encouragement that this book felt possible. And it is because they have let me into their lives and given me the privilege of witnessing their struggles and joys that this book has depth.

For the most visionary ideas in this book I credit Rabbi Michael Lerner (who in turn credits them to Abraham Joshua Heschel and Karl Marx). Michael's guidance in my own spiritual journey has been invaluable.

He was the first to publish my writing and has been a teacher and a friend to me.

Many thanks to Richard Elliott Friedman, whose beautiful translation and commentary have helped shape my understanding and love of Torah.

I thank my father for asking me philosophical questions when I was a child (e.g., "How do you know you really exist?") and teaching me that I could question reality from the ground up. I thank my mother for gifting me with freedom from television.

Most vitally, I thank my husband, Jeff, whose love sustains me. And I thank my children, Miriam and Micah (who have been so patient with my long hours of work and so excited on my behalf), for giving me a reason to write this book.

Further Reading

Arnold, Johann Christoph. *Their Name Is Today: Reclaiming Childhood in a Hostile World*. Walden, NY: Plough Publishing House, 2014.

Baudrillard, Jean. *Simulations*. New York: Semiotext[e], Columbia University, 1983.

Bergoglio, Jorge Mario (Pope Francis). *Evangelii Gaudium* [The joy of the Gospel]. Apostolic exhortation, November 26, 2013. http://w2.vatican.va/content/francesco/en/apost_exhortations/documents/papa-francesco_esortazione-ap_20131124_evangelii-gaudium.html.

Bergoglio, Jorge Mario (Pope Francis). *Laudato Si'* [Praise be to you]: *On Care for Our Common Home*. The Vatican, 2015. http://w2.vatican.va/content/francesco/en/encyclicals/documents/papa-francesco_20150524_enciclica-laudato-si.html.

Diamond, Eliezer. "Torah Study." In *The Observant Life: The Wisdom of Conservative Judaism for Contemporary Jews*, edited by Martin Cohen. New York: The Rabbinical Assembly, 2012.

Dreher, Rod. *The Benedict Option: A Strategy for Christians in a Post-Christian Nation*. New York: Sentinel, 2017.

Friedman, Richard Elliott. *Commentary on the Torah*. San Francisco: HarperOne, 2003.

Gold, Shefa. *Torah Journeys: The Inner Path to the Promised Land*. Teaneck, NJ: Ben Yehuda Press, 2006.

Heschel, Abraham Joshua. *The Sabbath*. New York: Farrar, Straus Giroux, 1951.

Lerner, Michael. *Jewish Renewal: A Path to Healing and Transformation*. New York: Harper Perennial, 1995.

Lerner, Michael. *The Left Hand of God: Taking Back Our Country from the Religious Right*. New York: HarperCollins, 2006.

Marx, Karl. *Capital, Volume 1: A Critique of Political Economy*. 1867. Reprint, New York: Vintage Books, Random House, 1977.

Moe-Lobeda, Cynthia. *Resisting Structural Evil: Love as Ecological-Economic Vocation*. Minneapolis: Fortress Press, 2013.

New Zealand Catholic Bishops Conference. "Statement on Environmental Issues," September 1, 2006. http://www.catholic.org.nz/nzcbc/fx-view-article.cfm?ctype=BSART&loadref=83&id=62.

Rachels, James. "Killing and Letting Die." In *Encyclopedia of Ethics*. 2nd ed. Edited by Lawrence C. Becker and Charlotte B. Becker. New York: Routledge, 2001.

Schachter-Shalomi, Zalman. *First Steps to a New Jewish Spirit: Reb Zalman's Guide to Recapturing the Intimacy & Ecstasy in Your Relationship with God*. Woodstock, VT: Jewish Lights Publishing, 2003.

Shurpin, Yehuda. "Can I Donate My Kidney against My Parent's Wishes?" http://www.chabad.org/library/article_cdo/

aid/2472791/jewish/Can-I-Donate-My-Kidney-Against
-My-Parents-Wishes.htm.

Silberberg, Naftali. "The Ten Commandments: The Inside
Story." June 6, 2014. http://www.jewishpress.com/judaism/
holidays/the-ten-commandments-the-inside-story/2014/
06/06/.

Singer, Peter. "The Singer Solution to World Poverty." *New
York Times Magazine.* September 5, 1999.

Telushkin, Joseph. *A Code of Jewish Ethics, Volume 1: You Shall
Be Holy.* New York: Bell Tower, 2006.

Waskow, Arthur, ed. *Torah of the Earth: Exploring 4,000 Years
of Ecology in Jewish Thought,* vol. 1. Woodstock, VT: Jewish Lights Publishing, 2000.

Wolf, Naomi. *The Beauty Myth: How Images of Beauty Are
Used against Women.* New York: Harper Perennial, 2002.

Index

About the Author

ANA LEVY-LYONS is a writer and preacher serving as senior minister of First Unitarian Congregational Society in Brooklyn, a quickly growing urban Unitarian Universalist congregation. She holds a BA from Brown University and an M.Div. from the University of Chicago Divinity School.

Ana's work revolves around building a religious counterculture—a multifaith movement that redeploys traditional religious practices to address the urgent needs of our time. She comes to this work as a child of postmodernity, raised in a secular household and fully aware of religion's limitations and dangers. She also brings the insights from her own spiritual journey—a journey that connected her with her Jewish heritage, inspired years of study and practice in the Jewish Renewal movement, and led to her career as a religious leader.

She has a foot in two worlds: the world of secular humanism (with its critique of religion) and the world of religion (with its critique of spiritually impoverished modernity). This dual vision forms the basis of her work. It allows her to translate religious insights and disciplines in a way that inspires secular and not-yet-observant audiences. She makes the case for keeping commandments in our postmodern, postreligious era.

Ana's sermons and articles are published in *Quest for Meaning*, *Criterion* (a University of Chicago publication), *UU World*, and *Tikkun* magazine, where she is a contributing editor. She also writes her own blog exploring the concept of the religious counterculture. Her sermons have won numerous awards, including the Borden Sermon Award. She serves as co-chair of the Brooklyn Heights Interfaith Clergy Association and completed an eighteen-month fellowship with Greenfaith in religious environmental leadership.

She lives in Manhattan with her husband, Jeff, and her young children, Miriam and Micah.